MONTANA MURDERS

MONTANA MURDERS

NOTORIOUS AND VANISHED

BRIAN D'AMBROSIO

RIVERBEND
PUBLISHING

RIVERBEND
PUBLISHING

An imprint of Globe Pequot, the trade division of
The Rowman & Littlefield Publishing Group, Inc.
4501 Forbes Blvd., Ste. 200
Lanham, MD 20706
www.rowman.com

Distributed by NATIONAL BOOK NETWORK

British Library Cataloguing in Publication Information available

Library of Congress Cataloging-in-Publication Data available

ISBN 978-1-6063-9143-3 (paper : alk. paper)
ISBN 978-1-4930-8579-8 (electronic)

♾™ The paper used in this publication meets the minimum requirements of
American National Standard for Information Sciences—Permanence of Paper for
Printed Library Materials, ANSI/NISO Z39.48-1992.

To the victims and their families
Some are in prison, some are dead;
And none has read my books,
And yet my thought turns back to them . . .

— "THE CHUMS," THEODORE ROETHKE

CONTENTS

NOTES ON SOURCES

THE NARRATIVES, DESCRIPTIONS, and time lines used and referenced to construct the stories in this book have been furnished from a wide variety of vetted and weathered sources, including formal police reports, interviews with authorized investigators, conversations with relatives and friends of the victims, news summaries, and meetings with private investigators and journalists who worked the cases when they first unfolded. In certain cases, the suspects and the accused themselves have elected to answer questions and face scrutiny.

Most of the subjects in this book have spoken candidly and with gritty frankness, but in a few circumstances, sources have requested anonymity, perhaps either out of fear of prejudicing the case or retribution from unknown parties, or for some other unspecified rationale. In such cases, anonymity has been granted.

ACKNOWLEDGMENTS

THANK YOU to all the special people connected to these ill-fated and soul-tiring cases who have lent their time, knowledge, information, and precious trust and mental resolve to discuss and make clear some of the conditions and situations encompassing the private lives and the wretched ends of the vanished and murdered subjects.

SUSAN ELIZABETH PEARSON

VANISHED: MARCH 17, 1966
VANISHED FROM: MISSOULA

SHE WAS A YOUNG SCHOOLTEACHER, pretty, from a well-heeled family, and respectable—just the type of classic archetype who should not end up the way she did—and her case aroused much public interest for that very reason.

Her name was Susan Pearson, and she went missing under the hazy, cold skies of Missoula, Montana, on Thursday, March 17, 1966.

A native of Portland, Oregon, Pearson was a thirty-year-old graduate student and instructor at the University of Montana (UM). Described as a quiet, compelling woman, Pearson was working feverishly on a doctoral thesis and a series of anthropology essays and was equally busy administering and grading examinations for a business course she was teaching.

Multiple searches for Pearson proved futile, and her apartment was undisturbed by theft or vandalism, offering no overt evidence of criminal wrongdoing. Her car was later discovered abandoned outside a noisy bar on a noisy party block in downtown Missoula; her purse, keys, and some other belongings were stowed inside. Years later, bones were recovered in a wooded area south of Missoula and initially suspected to be those of Pearson. But that probability was soon blown apart. The media stopped putting up a squawk, and Susan Pearson

A native of Portland, Oregon, Susan Pearson was a 30-year-old graduate student and instructor at the University of Montana (UM). Described as a quiet, compelling woman, Pearson was working feverishly on a doctoral thesis and a series of anthropology essays and was equally busy administering and grading examinations for a business course she was teaching. She went missing under inscrutable circumstances in March 1966 and her case is considered the oldest active cold case in the state of Montana. COURTESY MISSOULA COUNTY SHERIFF'S DEPARTMENT/PUBLIC DOMAIN

vanished once again—this time from the black, bold crown of the news headlines.

Is Pearson's story one of tragic death and violence, a tale of innocence plucked and life arbitrarily closed, or did she simply vanish on her own accord without known reason?

DISTINGUISHED PEDIGREE OF VICTIM

SUSAN ELIZABETH PEARSON was born on October 1, 1935, into a distinguished pedigree, the daughter of David and Agatha Pearson, the eldest of three children. Her father was a prominent insurance agent in Portland; her grandfather was Democratic state senator Walter J. Pearson, a four-term stalwart who resigned in the middle of his fourth term in 1964 due to ill health.

In 1966, the smart, promising, reddish blonde, part-time instructor at UM was working toward completing her doctoral thesis through the University of Oregon. Divorced several years before, she'd been dedicating herself to her work, focusing on her career. After dealing with her ex-husband's dalliances, she had had one charmer too many in her life. She dabbled without any pretense of commitment—sometimes, her friends said, with people who weren't her social equals.

March came in with a snowstorm. People took that sort of thing for granted in Missoula that time of the year. In fact, it snowed more than thirty inches in March 1966. Just what date in March Pearson was last seen isn't known; several sources claim Wednesday, March 16, and others Thursday, March 17. Some newspaper sources incorrectly use Sunday, March 13, as the date. Most likely it was March 17, several friends having claimed to have seen her on the University of Montana campus on that Thursday.

Friday, March 18, 1966. The city was cold that day, and there was no moon. The sky was clouded, without stars. It was the time when spring in Montana seemed like a cruel mirage, and no one felt as if they should be outside. Susan was scheduled to administer a business administration exam, but she failed to arrive. Twenty-four hours earlier, she had been on the same campus, huddled inside the warmth of the buildings, talking, wearing slacks, a green car coat with plaid lining, and two diamond rings. Her short hair was worn straight, and her brown eyes shifted with the conversations. Someone said that the last time that they saw her, her stride was "brisk" and "nervous."

Virtually no information appeared in the press about Susan within the first forty-eight hours of her disappearance. It took several days for the Missoula police to issue an all-points bulletin seeking information regarding her whereabouts. Nancy King, "a tall, blonde nightclub singer," according to published accounts, a friend of Pearson's, told law enforcement that Pearson had visited her a few days before and stated that she seemed to be in an "extremely nervous, evasive, and depressed condition." "It was just a totally different Sue," King told the police. King also alleged that Pearson had told her in the past that she had considered leaving and starting a new life.

Other friends, however, denied that she had any overt or seemingly abrupt emotional problems. They said that she never withdrew or seemed out of touch with reality, and nothing in her perusal of the world disturbed them. "King was a crackpot anyhow," one of them told investigators.

Soon after the bulletin was released, Pearson's vehicle was found parked on a side street not far from the UM campus, where police found her purse in plain sight, her car keys on the driver's side floorboard, and her driver's license and college ID badge in the console. A wallet with more than $100 dollars stuffed inside was found in the glove compartment, along with the usual paraphernalia: gloves, handkerchiefs, half-used packages of different brands of cigarettes, insurance papers, a woman's compact.

Police also learned that two checks in the name of Susan Pearson from her college employer totaling $1,200 were left unclaimed. Because they were never cashed, some speculated that this was proof that she hadn't left of her own accord.

INVESTIGATION YIELDS LITTLE EVIDENCE, ABUNDANCE OF SPECULATION

PEARSON LIVED ALONE. Upon inspection of her efficiency one-bedroom apartment at 160 Strand Avenue, police concluded that nothing appeared to be disturbed or vandalized. When they arrived, they were greeted by her brother David. Records—folk music, protest music, psychedelic disco—were neatly stacked in small piles on the floor and living room table, suggesting comfort rather than chaos. On the Salvation Army store couch, a copy of Simon and Garfunkel's *Homeward Bound* was removed from its sleeve.

Police inventoried and recorded some of the things that they had discovered: plastic barrettes that had fallen into the green shag carpet, plastic barrettes in a jar with marbles, rusty paper clips, and orphaned keys. "Nothing troubling," wrote one detective in his notes. A half-smoked package of Camels was on the table. Even good-looking women smoked back then. When she was extra nervous, Nancy would rub her cigarette end back and forth in the ashtray.

Weeks later, however, David told the Associated Press that it appeared to him as though his sister had "exited in a hurry," as a teakettle had been left on the stove, and the boiler was on. He said that an exterior porch light—which Pearson typically had left on in the evenings—had been turned off.

Police started to explore the possibility that she had been hurt or abducted by a student who wished to avenge some perceived wrong. Nancy King told law enforcement that "one or two boys" who had received poor grades in one of the courses Pearson was teaching had "threatened to wreck her car." King was the only source on record raising this possibility.

On March 31, local police officers investigated a claim that Pearson had been sighted at the top of Lolo Pass, on foot, wandering in the heavy snow, but found no evidence that she had been there. Someone reported that they had seen her intoxicated, drinking alone at a hot, crowded Missoula bar.

In May 1966, Pearson's family hired Burleigh Allen, a former FBI agent and private sleuth from Billings, to investigate their daughter's disappearance. But Allen wasn't able to locate Pearson or gather enough conclusive evidence to lead investigators to the person who might have harmed her. Allen was quoted in one newspaper as saying that he was "oddly stumped."

One of the stranger news clippings about the case comes from the April 3, 1966, *Bozeman Daily Chronicle*, quoting the Missoula authorities as stating that Pearson is a "young woman who loves folk music and would probably attend functions featuring this type of entertainment" and that her speech was "rapid," she used "jive" talk, and her voice was "husky alto." Another article intimated that she had enough style or poise to attract the good men, but she had a way of going after the unsavory types.

Rumors—transmitted in the form of a large share of harsh, judgmental letters to the editor—swirled that she was killed after a hookup with a dangerous man, perhaps even a serial killer. One missive went so far as to insinuate that she had asked for her fate—and that a vengeful God, the letter writer theorized, had delivered it with fury.

But police said they had no reason to believe that to be true. On October 29, 1970, small, thin bones were discovered in the Blue Mountain area south of Missoula by several UM students on a field ecology trip. The sheriff who first examined the scene suspected they may have been dumped there several years before by "some ritualistic style killer," he said. Investigators initially supposed the bones belonged to the five-foot, ninety-seven-pound Pearson. However, the pathologist in charge declared that they were not human and, instead, belonged to a bear. Pathologist Dr. Buchanan said that the bone piles had too many irregularities and inconsistencies to be human, including larger wrist bones.

Missoula County Attorney Harold J. Pinsoneault stated after the discovery of the bones that it had been suspected that Pearson "may have been murdered in the Blue Mountain area," though he did not elaborate on this specific thread of reasoning or elucidate just what prompted such comment.

No suspect has ever been formally named or publicly attached by authorities to Susan Pearson's death. Susan's ex-husband was never considered a suspect, and he was formally investigated and cleared of suspicion.

Her disappearance most likely is the oldest cold case on active status in the state of Montana.

DOROTHY FREEMAN

VANISHED: SEPTEMBER 7, 1970
VANISHED FROM: WISDOM

ONE SUNDAY NIGHT in 1970, Dorothy Freeman, a twenty-six-year-old teacher, cooked a spaghetti dinner and made a series of phone calls to family members. She and her parents talked on into the night. She thumbed through a few magazines, including one *Life* and a couple of *National Geographics*. Her Missoula apartment was full of books. One entire wall of the living room was filled with bookshelves, and more shelves filled the entry alcove. Books were on bedside tables, magazines and newspapers in racks. She read books all the time. The schoolteacher read for pleasure, and she was never without a book in her hand.

Though late in the evening, she drank a cup of coffee. Perhaps she had been anxious about starting the new assignment in the morning. Earlier in the year she had been attending the University of Montana and had done some student teaching. But now she had taken on a bigger responsibility elsewhere, away from Missoula—and new tasks always bring new stresses. But after she drank her first cup of coffee boiling hot—she relaxed. At around 8 p.m., she pushed against the old wooden door of her apartment and, stepping into the invigorating late summer wind, she stepped outside. Warm currents of air blew across the Clark Fork River and settled on the city.

Dorothy climbed into the green and white 1960 Ford Fairlane that she owned, a gorgeous piece of machinery with a horizontal fin that stretched the entire length of the body, capped with a chrome accent trim. It only got maybe fifteen miles a gallon, but it sure was slick. It was like a piece of sculptural art, her prize possession, and it was parked in front of the new apartment development. After getting in the car, she fidgeted with the mirrors, bolted the doors, and zigzagged a few blocks. In no time, she was at the city's edge, heading south on Highway 93, en route to the Bitterroot Valley.

What happened to her from there is a decades-old mystery.

FAIRFIELD FARM GIRL

FREEMAN WAS "A QUIET GIRL," according to those who knew and loved her. She was "a friendly young woman," said another. She was polite and mild mannered, and she always paid her rent on time. She was "a good person," her coworkers went on, a good person without bad vices, and she had lots of friends.

A native of Fairfield, Dorothy grew up on a farm northeast of town, attended Greenfield Grade School, and graduated from Fairfield High School. Her daily chores consisted of helping with the grain crops and raising animals, including cattle, pigs, and chickens. Dorothy had always wished to become a schoolteacher—a job that perhaps was the personification of her innocence. She enjoyed her studies at the University of Montana and, even though far from home, always expressed a willingness to talk with her parents, with whom she was exceptionally close. She talked to them several times a week on the telephone, not long but enough to express a sense of her warmth and fondness. When a teaching job emerged in the Bitterroot Valley, she was buoyed by the prospects of a fulfilled dream.

MISSING, YET SEEN FOUR TIMES

FREEMAN WAS SUPPOSED to show up Monday, September 7, 1970, for a teaching job in Hamilton. Alas, police records about the case are scant, and the exact school or the nature of the job was never identified in their limited accounts. Why she left on Sunday night instead of rising early and commuting the following day, and exactly where she planned to spend the night, has never been explained or reported.

When she didn't arrive, the class was canceled, and phone calls were made to the woman's residence. That night Dorothy's parents were contacted, and in turn, the Missoula police were summoned to the residence. There was no indication that she had left in a hurry or hastily, or that anything had been packed, stored, or was missing. The place looked tidy and well appointed. Cash was on the kitchen table, and police later learned that she had left money behind in three separate bank accounts. A large amount of meat was stored in a stand-alone locker, and the cupboards were teeming with canned goods and sundries.

The Missoula police discovered close to nothing in the missing woman's background to suggest that she would be a candidate for foul play or one who would stage or fake her own disappearance. They located her friends, her acquaintances, and tried to ascertain when or where a stranger could fit in. Nothing about the woman suggested that she had anything troubling in her life to run away from.

Authorities were even more flummoxed after the missing woman was purportedly seen about four times. Someone said that she was seen the next afternoon at a Wisdom café, seventy-four miles southeast of Hamilton. Others reported she was spotted the following day, Tuesday, September 8, 1970, at a cafe at Wise River east of Wisdom and again, later that day, back in the Wisdom area.

Freeman's half brother, Orville Grasdock, was the origin source of the Wisdom café sighting. Orville told police that he talked to a Hamilton woman who said that Dorothy left the cafe and traveled three miles toward Hamilton before turning around and heading back toward Wisdom. Grasdock told authorities that the witness gave an exact description of his sister—five feet eight, 150 pounds, with fair skin, blue eyes, and brown hair—and her two-tone 1960 Ford.

The final of the four alleged sightings was attributed to a heavy equipment operator in Beaverhead County who told authorities that he was certain that he had observed Dorothy driving along Montana Highway 43, between Wisdom and Wise River. If it was her, it would be the final time she would ever be seen.

Approximately forty miles of paved road through a huge, raw, lonely country connects Wisdom with the Wise River, and in the early 1970s it was not a heavily traveled highway. The lonely stretch wends through parts of the Beaverhead National Forest and the Anaconda-Pintlar Wilderness area. Local and state law enforcement officers carried out a ground and air search of the region. Tracking dogs were summoned to sniff out any trace of Freeman's whereabouts. A nationwide police teletype alert was issued.

WICKED TOLL TAKEN ON PARENTS

DOROTHY FREEMAN'S VANISHING inflicted a brutal toll on her parents, Herman and Gertrude Spoelder Grasdock. Herman Grasdock spent his spare time combing back roads in the Hamilton, Wisdom, and Wise River areas and even searched the area by helicopter. He spent weekends, holidays, and summer breaks driving dusty roads, peering in the backyards of ranches, gazing down into dark gullies and ravines, hoping to find some indication of his daughter's whereabouts. He drove all the main roads and secondary ones in Ravalli County. His mind swirling around like a backwater eddy, he even traveled to Idaho and throughout the Northwest.

Herman told the media that Dorothy was especially close to her parents, and one local newspaper mentions that Dorothy was in Fairfield one weekend in May 1970 to visit them and celebrate Herman's birthday.

Herman also hired a helicopter and searched the Skalkaho Pass area between Hamilton and Anaconda. As beautiful as it all was, the mountains, the rivers, the remote expanses—these places no longer held any air of happiness or peace of mind. The savagery and the brutality of the experience wrecked his mind and body. For Herman, the search for his daughter ended in 1972 when he suffered a stroke that physicians believe was induced by acute stress. A subsequent stroke left him paralyzed, and he was confined to the Teton County Nursing Home in Choteau. Half his face drooped badly; his mobility stolen from him, at times Herman could barely muster the vocal strength to speak his lost daughter's name. His nurses served as his translators.

In 1972, Gertrude Grasdock told the media that she had her hopes up "many times" that her daughter would be found alive and safe. But nothing came of it, and she didn't know "what to think." She said she once believed that Dorothy was suffering from amnesia and that the missing child would one day reappear. The Grasdocks' sons and other daughters and their children spent Thanksgiving and Christmas and most of the other holidays with their parents. Their lost loved one was never far from their minds.

"We talked about it but couldn't think of anything more to do than has already been done," said Gertrude in 1972. "I just keep taking care of my husband, and Orville keeps on with his farm work."

Two years later, Gertrude referred to the odd, inexplicable violence in the state, which was afterward determined to be the work of the heinous David Meirhofer. "With all these kidnappings going on, you kind of wonder if that's what happened."

Vera Grasdock, sister-in-law of Dorothy Freeman, told one local newspaper that at first, she believed that the woman had impulsively decided to explore or take a trip without notifying the family. "We thought at first she might have just gone off to be by herself," she said to the *Havre Daily News*. "But after three years we don't think so."

Vera described her sister-in-law as a "quiet, reserved woman" who decided to go to college in 1968 after learning that her husband, stationed with the Air Force in Thailand, had filed for divorce. In 1963, Dorothy, then nineteen, married Jimmie E. Freeman, twenty-one, a serviceman at the Malmstrom Air Force Base.

Gertrude said that her daughter resented the way she was treated during the brief marriage, how she was cast aside as if she were nothing, how he had moved on so quickly to another relationship without the slightest consideration of her. She said that Dorothy had always been "responsible" and "deeply religious," but the divorce had left her a different person, plodding along in her own little ruts. Plagued with severe stress headaches and occasional choking fits, she would often lie awake at night for hours and dream fitfully when she slept. She frequently came to her mother and said she'd had a bad dream.

"She was concerned about her divorce and several other things," Gertrude said, "but she wasn't the type of person to just take off and never let us know."

Eventually, public interest in the case eroded. Though family members were still willing to talk, there was never anything new to report or new to express. How many times could they repeat how much they missed her dearly? As time passed, they wanted to maintain as much privacy as they could. But when pressed about Dorothy, the Grasdock family told of the pain the drama caused everyone.

"Everybody would like to know what happened to Dorothy," Gertrude Grasdock told the *Fairfield Current*. "If we just knew one way or the other it would relieve a lot of tension and worry. We still hope that someday something will turn up one way or the other."

NO SIGN OF 1960 FAIRLANE 500 FORD

DOROTHY'S PRIZED VEHICLE was never located, and perhaps the slimmest chance still exists that someday it could miraculously emerge at an estate sale or car show or antique road show. The 1960 Fairlane 500 Ford is a four-door sedan with Montana license number 31-315 and identification serial number OP42X 128 923.

Herman Grasdock died in 1974, "bringing to an end the torment of his daughter's disappearance in 1970," his obituary began morosely. Dorothy's mother, Gertrude, died in 1991. Jimmie E. Freeman was determined to be stationed overseas at the time of Dorothy's disappearance, and he was not considered a suspect.

DONNA LEMON

LAST SEEN: BOZEMAN

FOUND MURDERED: JULY 9, 1973, IDAHO FALLS, IDAHO

THE SNAKE RIVER IS A behemoth marvel of nature with mouths, bridges, and inlets that encompass more than a thousand miles across parts of six states. Originating from a series of small headwaters in the Rocky Mountains of western Wyoming, it cuts its vast, tangled mark through southern Idaho, including Idaho Falls, a city in Bonneville County.

On Monday, July 9, 1973, at approximately 7:42 p.m., the body of a young woman was discovered near the river's greenish-blue shoreline, a sunny, radiant sky above. The falling rays of the evening sun streamed through the trees off Milligan Road, lighting a wooded area where, about fifteen feet from the edge of the tributary and several steps from the road, a local man spotted a heavy, awkward lump in the ankle-high scrub.

Closer inspection revealed the bloody and begrimed features of a prostrate Caucasian female with light brown hair, dark frame glasses, about five feet, seven inches tall, and weighing about 110 pounds. Though fully clothed, the body was an unsightly mash of cuts, slashes, and bruises, the metallic tang of caked blood emanating from it. Her throat cut, she bled to death after the main artery in her neck was severed.

The victim was stabbed multiple times, though knife wounds on the woman's right side "were apparently not deep

GALLATIN COUNTY SHERIFF'S DEPARTMENT
BOZEMAN, MONTANA 59715
L.D.W. ANDERSON, Sheriff

MISSING PERSON

Request any help or information you can give us on above subject missing from Gallatin County since 7-5-73.

DONNA IRENE LEMON — WFA — Age 20 — DOB 11-6-1952 — 5'7'' — 110 Lbs. — Medium length blond hair (slightly longer than photo) — Dark frame glasses — Right leg scarred by acid — Normally wears western type clothing. Subject has weak left eyelid.

Subject was last seen by a friend approximately 3:00 P.M., July 5, 1973. Her car is described as a 1969 green Mustang hardtop, Montana Lic. # 6-9661. The right rear bumper on this vehicle is bent.

Any information please contact the Gallatin County Sheriff's Dept. Call collect 406-586-2315.

Donna Lemon, twenty, was a Bozeman, Montana, nurse who vanished after stopping in a convenience store in Gallatin Canyon in 1973. Days later, she was found murdered close to the Snake River in Idaho.

enough to have mortally wounded her," according to a later coroner's report. No determination was rendered regarding whether she was sexually assaulted. Details were scarce, though Sheriff Blaine Skinner told the media that he believed the kill site was the location where the body was discovered.

A pair of prescription glasses and a green 1969 Ford Mustang nearby identified the victim as Montana resident Donna Irene Lemon. Later, dental records were also traced and matched to her.

Donna's vehicle was located off Broadway in Idaho Falls, where it was "parked inconspicuously for several days" about one mile from where its owner was found; its doors were unlocked, and some of its contents were strewn across the dashboard and seats. It yielded a smattering of patches of dried blood "by the driver's door handle and on a shift handle," according to police records.

A pair of prescription glasses and a green 1969 Ford Mustang nearby identified the victim as Montana resident Donna Irene Lemon. Later, dental records were also matched to her. Though DNA technology was in its embryonic stages, a partial palm print and a number of fingerprints were preserved. COURTESY AUTHOR'S COLLECTION

Though DNA technology was still in its embryonic stages, a partial palm print and a number of fingerprints were preserved.

Before long, investigators were to determine that the victim was a well-liked young lady who was "quiet, happy and fun, without a mean bone in her body," as one friend recalled her. Donna was from a well-grounded family and was born and raised in the Gallatin Canyon. At the time, she was a twenty-year-old nurse living in Bozeman, Montana, a city roughly two hundred miles north of where her life ended abruptly along the shore of the Snake River in eastern Idaho.

With interstate coordination in the early 1970s a bit haphazard, authorities in two states investigated many possibilities, though largely separately, to determine the woman's trail to Idaho and who had brutally ended her life. Combined, they chased hundreds of tips, which led them down a number of frustrating cul-de-sacs.

To date, all the hard work by Montana and Idaho authorities has proven futile. The case of Donna Lemon's death has remained unsolved for forty-eight years.

ROOTS IN THE GALLATIN CANYON

DAUGHTER OF George and Clara Lou Lemon, Donna Irene Lemon was born November 7, 1952, and lived most of her life in the Gallatin Canyon, about forty-five miles south of Bozeman. George, a former military engineer in the army's Tenth Mountain Division, was an avid outdoorsman with a particular zeal for rock climbing, skiing, and horse packing trips. George married Clara Lou Barnes in 1950, and they lived in the home built from logs that George sawed with his own muscle. To support his family, George worked for the Montana State Highway Department.

Donna was a quiet child, the first of George and Clara Lou's two daughters along with her younger sister, Verna. From the earliest age, Donna is described as smart, disciplined, and kind, someone who loved animals and had inherited her father's passion for remote places and physically challenging adventures. The Lemon girls were always surrounded by dogs, cats, or horses, and Donna and Verna would sometimes ensnare chipmunks in fox traps and keep them as pets for a while before turning them loose or until they escaped back into the woods. Among their many frequent outdoor experiences, George regularly took Donna rock climbing—some old, thick ropes strung off a cliff, nothing too extreme, just enough excitement to ensure a safe descent and enliven the senses.

The family rode horses together, repeatedly embarking on pack and multiday camping trips, crates of food and other critical supplies in tow, to the azure lakes in the Spanish Peaks mountain range in the Gallatin Canyon. Donna was a bold rider, always cool and fearless, and eager to ride all day.

"Donna was an avid backcountry skier, too," says Verna Sene, Donna's sister. "We would take off at night and go backcountry skiing in the moonlight. She loved rock climbing. Dad was good at that, too, and he pursued it with her. Fishing, camping, hunting—she loved the outdoors. We killed elk and deer."

Patricia Barnes Conway is Donna Lemon's first cousin. At the time that Donna was killed, Patricia was sixteen years old and staying with George, Clara Lou, and Verna for the week and working at Buck's T-4.

"I admired her," says Patricia. "She was a lot like the mother hen, and she watched out for the younger ones, and she had a maternal instinct to her. She was a loving, caring, quiet person, and she had a good sense of humor. Her and her dad had a very close relationship. In the woods, we'd go out hunting, where she was like a cat; she could sneak up on you, and you would not know that she was coming. Our families spent every holiday together. Snowmobiling in the wintertime. We kids would be gone for hours. We'd go sledding behind their house [the Lemons], or we snowshoed."

Donna attended the Ophir school in the Gallatin Canyon (now called the Big Sky School District #72) from kindergarten through eighth grade before traveling to Bozeman to complete junior high and high school.

"When we lived up in the Gallatin, few residents lived there year 'round," says Verna Sene. "Ranches and dude ranches up and down the canyon were main attractions at that time. Our Ophir School had eight kids in all eight grades, a one-room school with a little cabin out back that the teacher lived in to stay right there. "Lots of times we had to go outside to the outhouse, and there would be moose in the yard, and we couldn't get to the bathrooms."

At Bozeman High School, Donna was a member of the Girls' Rifle Club—a yearbook photo shows a determined Donna taking aim at target practice—where she earned a reputation as a good marksman and a crack shot, even pocketing a few medals from competitions. After graduating in 1971, Donna spent two years working to obtain a degree at Montana State University as a licensed practical nurse. As a refuge from studying, she whittled away stress at the shooting range at the university.

In the summer of 1973, Donna was employed full-time as a nurse at Bozeman Health Deaconess Hospital, where she routinely worked the evening shift. She also worked a second job as a housekeeper at the Castle Rock Inn.

The girl from the Gallatin Canyon was now her own woman, embracing real-world responsibilities: tall and slender, her brown hair was neatly clipped, and she had a face marked with a pair of blue-gray eyes, a modest smile, and a calm, dignified expression that unfailingly inspired trust and respect. Though a heavily lidded left eye caused her instinctively to deflect her body position to the right, she was for the most part self-confident.

In July 1973, Donna had just moved out of living quarters with her roommate, Diane Mihalovich, on the west end of Bozeman when Diane got married. Donna's pleasant, single-bedroom apartment on tree-lined Willson Avenue was closer to her employment at the hospital and adjacent to MSU, where she planned to enroll in classes in the fall that would allow her to advance as a registered nurse.

"Donna was quiet, sweet, and very trusting," says Mihalovich.

"She went into the perfect profession for her," says Donna's friend Sherry Pierce, "because she was such a caring individual. I was younger by a couple of years, but we became fast friends. . . . We would go horseback riding, fishing, and do lots of outdoor activities. Her folks raised her that way; I'd been raised that way."

A MYSTERY DISAPPEARANCE

WHILE POLICE INVESTIGATORS have grappled with the task of reconstructing the victim's last days, they are certain that on the evening of Tuesday, July 3, and the afternoon of Wednesday, July 4, 1973, Donna Lemon and Sherry Pierce attended the Ennis rodeo together. Around the sights of kicking horses and clenching cowboys, Donna was smiling and relaxed. When a song from the Statler Brothers, or Gordon Lightfoot, or Johnny Cash erupted through the speakers (Pierce says Jack Blanchard and Misty Morgan's "Tennessee Bird Walk" always brought a spurt of enthusiasm from her), Donna was a paragon of contentment.

The following day, Thursday, July 5, the two friends had made plans to go horseback riding in the Gallatin Canyon sometime after 4 p.m.

"Her folks lived five or six miles from where we lived," says Sherry. "We lived right on West Fork Creek, a mile up the road, where we leased some property and had four or five head of horses, and that's where we were planning to go. We were going to meet at my house and then go there."

On July 5, sometime after 11 a.m., Donna stopped at the Corral Bar and met her sister Verna for hamburgers and bottles of Coke. Later, she reportedly was seen by the mother of one of her friends at the Standard station on West Main in Bozeman alongside her Mustang, a vehicle she had recently acquired at Ford's garage on the trade-in of a Chevrolet Bel Air. Donna made eye contact, and the two exchanged smiles and waves.

At approximately 1 p.m., Donna picked up her paycheck of $316.80 at Bozeman Deaconess Hospital and stopped at Security Bank & Trust Co., in Bozeman, where she received $116.80 back in cash.

Police also believe that Donna went to Monarch's Clothing Store at Buttrey's shopping center in Bozeman, where she bumped into her cousin Patricia. Patricia was there with her mother and sister. Donna was alone. The Lemon family had plans to attend a family reunion in Moscow, Idaho, the weekend of July 7 and 8, expecting to leave on Friday, July 6. For the occasion, Donna looked for new clothes, perhaps a special pair of jeans or a studded knit top.

"Donna came in and said that she was getting ready for the reunion," says Patricia. "Her and my sister tried on things in the dressing room together, and I think she bought a white shirt. I know she was trying some shirts on. She was going to pick up her paycheck and then go to the bank. . . . She mentioned that she was going to be meeting a friend to go horseback riding at 4 p.m. That was the last I saw of her . . ."

"Donna was planning to go out to pick up her paycheck and do something at the new apartment," says Pierce. "She was planning to then head back up the canyon, where we would squeeze in a horseback ride in the early evening. Then she'd finish packing. Leave the next day to go to Idaho."

It is not known if Donna visited her apartment. Witness accounts, however, place Donna at Stacey's Old Faithful Bar and Steakhouse, at 300 Mill Street, in Gallatin Gateway, at between roughly 2:30 and 4 p.m. There, according to bartender Jean Holland, Donna entered the bar, ordered a single can of Olympia to go, paid with a $1 bill, received the change, and then left. This transaction, which from start to finish lasted no more than five minutes, remains the last known or confirmed public sighting of Donna Lemon.

Patty Wells, a young woman from Gallatin Gateway, told police she believed she saw Donna driving east toward Highway 191. Wells did not see anyone else in the vehicle with Lemon.

"Her favorite thing to do was to drive up Gallatin Valley," recalls Donna's friend and former roommate, Diana Mihalovich. "She would sit by the river and have a beer and smoke a cigarette, and contemplate life, and then head on home. Something I have thought that she might have done on the day she was last seen."

She never arrived at Pierce's place for the horseback ride, nor did she stop in before the ride to visit with her parents nearby.

Sherry Pierce called Donna's house, did not receive a response, and someone told her that her friend had not been seen by George or Clara Lou that evening, either. Pierce, heightened by a sense of unease, jumped into her car and started driving around the community. A few hours later, Sherry contacted Donna's folks again. She remembers driving around with her friend's increasingly concerned parents for several hours, well into the dark.

"The next day," says Pierce, "we drove the canyon again because we thought she might've driven off of the road in an obscure place."

"We knew something was wrong," says Donna's sister Verna, "though the protocol of law enforcement for someone Donna's age was that she probably had a fight with her boyfriend or that she had run off with a boyfriend—not to deal with it right away."

CHASING SUSPECTS

FOR NEARLY FIVE DECADES, authorities have tried to follow the violent path that brought the jovial, gentle-spirited Donna Lemon from a life she loved in Bozeman, Montana, to such a grisly death hundreds of miles away in Idaho Falls.

"There were a lot of out-of-state workers in the area at Big Sky," says Sherry Pierce, "a lot of people from out of town, or who weren't local, from other places in the state. But I've always felt that because it was up close and personal, and because the circumstances of the car and location and other things surrounding it, that it was someone she knew."

From the beginning of the investigation, Idaho authorities considered that few people were killed in such a gruesome fashion by someone they had no acquaintance with.

But they entertained the notion that Donna's death could be the work of serial killer David Meirhofer, who committed four horrific random murders in the Bozeman area between 1967 and 1974, before determining that Meirhofer had no part in Donna's death.

Contract workers with transient ties to the building and expansion of the Big Sky Ski Resort were investigated, as were factory workers at nearby Gallatin Gateway Cheese Factory.

"The area was a booming place for transients and seasonal workers at the time," says Detective Mike Hammer of the Bonneville County Police Department. "The time frame of that summertime shows a big influx, a lot of people who could have come and gone, or who could have been there, and no one could have known."

As is common procedure in a murder investigation, police probed Donna's relationship history; there was no husband to question, though she had dated casually over the years and was seeing a man named Gary Scheidecker at the time of her death.

Scheidecker, who worked as a security guard at Big Sky Resort in the summer of 1973 and later worked at the Gallatin County Sheriff's Office, says that to the best of his recollection, he was away on military leave at the time of Donna's abduction. Though police reports place Scheidecker and his friend Ric Brown at the same rodeo event that Donna attended the evening before she was last seen, Scheidecker says that he doesn't recall the exact day or time that he last saw Donna.

"It was a while . . . it might have been sometime before she died, I don't know," says Gary Scheidecker. "I was interviewed by the FBI right afterwards. I don't remember much about her. All I know was that she was supposed to meet a friend after stopping at Stacey's."

There was also one local Gallatin Gateway man around Donna's age who seemed to be especially obsessed by her. Police identified and homed in on him and even members of his family, though none have ever been charged in connection to the crime.

Although plausible theories exist involving the possibility of a serial killer or a random attacker, no one who knew Donna believes that she would have let a stranger in her vehicle. Donna was last seen in Bozeman on July 5, but her car was first observed by an Idaho Falls police officer working the night shift on July 7, 1973, two days before its owner was discovered. The whereabouts of Donna and the vehicle on July 6, 1973, are unknown.

"It is hard to imagine that Donna would have stopped willingly to give someone a ride on the highway unless she knew them," says Verna Sene.

Shortly after Donna's murder, the FBI assisted local authorities in the identification and processing of the various fingerprints that were powdered and pulled from the interior of Donna's vehicle.

"The FBI told me then that they were damn sure that Donna's killer was someone that she and we knew," says Pierce. "They were cautioning me and concerned for my safety and felt that I could alert this person in some fashion, and that I may become on this person's list. At the time, I was afraid."

Many questions surrounding the uncharted details of Donna's death still haunt the investigation. Was the murder scene indeed in Idaho Falls or was Donna killed in the Bozeman area?

"I would say that she was likely killed in Idaho Falls," says Detective Mike Hammer. "There is no reason to believe that she was leaving to come to Idaho Falls or it was a destination.

It's likely the killer or killers were in the car when she got to Idaho Falls. Nothing says that it had to be one person or that it wasn't more than one. . . . There was just enough decomposition and bloating that would hide some of that stuff that we would be very interested in knowing."

Hammer refers to DNA technology, namely the partial samples collected from the Mustang almost a half century ago, that might help unravel the secrets shrouding Donna's murder.

In 2009, the Bonneville County Sheriff's Office announced that they had DNA samples to work with and said they had identified three men as potential suspects. The testing using the new DNA technology cleared one of the suspects from the pool. According to the January 2009 press release, another test was being applied to the DNA of the second suspect (it failed to match), and the third suspect still needed to be tracked down by authorities and be tested.

"We had the crude DNA profile of a male, but nobody that could be tied to it," says Mike Hammer.

SEARCH FOR RESOLUTION

FOR MANY YEARS George and Clara Lou watched helplessly while the investigation of the brutal death of their beloved daughter petered into oblivion; they had no ability to avenge their loss, no remedy but tears.

"No one seems to be able to come up with an answer to our questions," Clara Lou once said to the press. "Who and why? Somewhere, someone knows these answers. Will they ever be answered for us?"

Both George and Clara Lou Lemon died without ever knowing the hard facts of their child's fate.

"The truth is that we don't know what happened to Donna," says Detective Hammer. "There were multiple suspects and possibilities that made them likely. Stats show that most people are killed by someone close to them. But it could have been a stranger."

Hammer says that it is confounding that such a terrible crime could happen in an area as insular as Gallatin Gateway was in the 1970s without tongues sooner or later loosening. "It's hard to believe that in a close-knit community like Bozeman was in 1973 that nothing has ever come up. We are hoping that someone could provide that one lead or that one new thought or spark that connects the dots for us."

Despite the disappointment of dead ends, Donna's family and friends are not doomed to thinking that the killer will forever escape identification or that an arrest in this crime is out of the question. "Donna's murder was earth shattering to a lot of people," says Patricia Barnes Conway. "And it still is."

Forty miles south of Bozeman on the grounds at Soldiers Chapel Cemetery on the West Fork of the Gallatin River, a memorial fountain engraved in Donna Lemon's memory was erected a few years after she was murdered. The inscription reads: "In loving memory of our friend, Donna Irene Lemon, 1952–1973. By Gallatin Canyon young people."

FRANCES EWALT

VANISHED: AUGUST 19, 1973
VANISHED FROM: FORSYTH

FORSYTH, MONTANA. Approximately 11 p.m., August 19, 1973. The street was cold, but the Agate Bar was hot and crowded. A mist of smoke hung in the air like smog and people, back to back, hip to hip, filled the space between the door and the bar, the bar and jukebox. In the back, the tables in the long, narrow room were full, and by midnight the air was almost rancid. There were parties at every booth, drinkers four deep at the billiards table. Happy-tail women were bouncing out of their dresses on the bar stools. Neon lights flashed inside of the bar and out. The pink neon sign over the entrance blinked monotonously. The joint showed no signs of closing.

Frances Ewalt stepped outside of the Agate Bar and looked both ways into the dark on Main Street. It had rained all summer, and there were billions of mosquitoes. There was the smell of dust and sage in the clear air. She said good-bye to a female friend, Jackie Love, and told her that she was going to see her younger brother, Gary Collier, an aspiring musician, at another bar, nearby. She said that she was going to walk to it. According to Gary, she never arrived.

She was never seen or heard from again.

One August night in 1973, Frances Ewalt, a young mother of three, stepped outside of the Agate Bar in Forsyth where she had been socializing and conversing amiably. She looked both ways into the dark on Main Street. Though she told friends that she was going to walk to another bar close by, she was never seen or heard from again. PHOTO COURTESY ROSEBUD COUNTY SHERIFF'S OFFICE

MUSSELSHELL COUNTY FARM GIRL

DAUGHTER OF Marion Faye Collins and Lee Roy Collier, Frances was born April 25, 1949, in Melstone. She was the quintessential Musselshell County farm girl, tomboyish, snap-button shirts, long, sparkling cowboy boots. She never strayed too far from the small town where she was raised. She married a man named Daniel Ewalt. Daniel, a native of Wibaux, Montana, and Frances were married on August 5, 1967, in Custer County, listing 224 South Fifth Street, Miles City, as the address on their marriage registration.

By all accounts, the marriage was ill-fated, tense, and fraught with problems from the onset. Daniel's first marriage had ended badly—and recently, in April 1967. People said Daniel was irritable and restless, and he seemed "unstable." He was drinking as much as a quart of Seagrams a day. Perhaps he felt trapped. Trapped in marriage. Trapped with three young children. Trapped by his own heavy drinking.

In the throes of a pending divorce that she was pursuing, Frances dug down deep; life had been hard, but she didn't cry, she didn't even say that she was hurt. She decided to fix her life for the better and for the betterment of her children. She found a job as a cocktail waitress and was said to have loved it. The extra work at the Century Club in Forsyth would provide the chance for her to earn extra money—and for that she was grateful. Indeed, she was determined to try her hardest to make the best of what she had, in a sad but proud, guilt-free way.

A SMALL-TOWN LOCAL VANISHES

THERE IS A COMMUNITY of life in itsy-bitsy Forsyth, and surely the Colliers were part of it. Despite the long, dirt road stretches between neighbors, the bonds between them are secure, close up, and sealed. On July 4, 1973, Frances's family recall a happy time, a table of seniors dressed in Western garb, string ties, cowboy shirts, jeans on the men and women, all coal miners' daughters, wearing fancy lampshade-shaped skirts and dirndl tops. They were full, fat, and tired. The day made known all the hot weather trademarks of summer: swimming pools and meaty barbecues and yard sales. One of Frances's relatives remembers even to this day what her favorite dish was: creamed herring, dill pickles, limburger cheese, and pumpernickel bread.

Only a few weeks after Frances disappeared, part of the town crashed and broke and began to cry. Most of the locals believed that the small town had experienced more than just a missing person—it was involved in a very serious murder. Everybody listened for gossip and watched closely for suspicious behavior.

FAMILY SUSPECTED SOMETHING SINISTER ALL ALONG

FEW PEOPLE BELIEVED that Frances would willingly leave behind three small boys. And she left behind more than just the most precious things in her world; she also left behind her most recent paycheck, all her hard-earned and hard-fought money sitting in the bank, and every shred of the clothing that she wasn't wearing hanging in her closet.

And on top of this, she left behind a mother, a frantic parent who tried to convince the community that her daughter was no footloose young woman out rendezvousing. "Frances wouldn't leave without telling us," Marion told the local television station. Marion's hopes of seeing her daughter again grew dimmer with each passing day; by the time the end of the year presented itself, she was weighed down by a terrible pessimism.

"We were afraid of foul play from the beginning, but when there was no word from her at Christmas, we knew something terrible had happened to her," she said in 1974.

Despite the harsh totality of the circumstances, as well as a gnawing, bitter sense of gloom, Marion and Leo Collier continued their search for clues to the mystery of her disappearance.

"I'll bet she's at the bottom of the river," said Marion, a bleak reference to the July 1974 murder of Peggy Harstad, a twenty-one-year-old Rosebud girl who was attacked and drowned by two drifting hitchhikers. Harstad made the fatal mistake of picking up the despicable sickos while they were roving aimlessly in eastern Montana, following a string of burglaries in the Midwest.

According to her parents, Frances talked of two things before her disappearance: a pending divorce and plans to take her sons to the Rosebud County Fair. How could it possibly be that no one had seen her after she left the Agate Bar? Her car was parked on a side street. The windows were open. Many of her children's toys and stuffed animals were on the back seat. She took motherhood seriously. She had a lifetime of memories to live on and many, many more to create. None of it made the least bit of sense. And that senselessness left the family with an awful collective sense of dread.

"Why can't anyone do anything?" her mother asked.

Sheriff James Scriffer said he wished that he could do more than what he'd dutifully done. He said that his men had interviewed friends, relatives, and others who knew the missing woman. Daily, he thumbed through missing persons reports. He said that he scoured the countryside and hunted down numerous leads that, in the end, only proved too vague and too insubstantial. Nothing. Nothing. Nothing. He emphasized the lack of results.

Frances's family members asked the police to continue to investigate Daniel Ewalt, to locate him and interrogate him, to put him at the top in terms of priority. He'd gotten in some kind of fight with Frances in her apartment recently, and she had considered pressing charges. Perhaps he was angry with her and had gone after her again? The police responded publicly to the Colliers' emotional pleas, expressing their deepest sympathies, but they'd spoken with Daniel, and he was very calm and very cooperative. We don't think that he could ever be vindictive toward your daughter, they said. Marion was incredulous. They hustled him in and out of there pretty quickly, she said. Too quickly for her taste.

Brother Charles Collier made several public statements in the spring of 1974. "She took nothing with her," he said. "You know, it takes money to go anywhere. She didn't take any money with her." Charles mentioned that in a Billings bank, a trust fund established for Frances by her grandfather had not been touched.

In her final interview on record, Marion Collier sat at her kitchen table and described what had been transpiring in her mind, gruesome and haunting images of her daughter's demise. "Knifed. Raped. All of those thoughts enter your mind."

POSSIBLE PEGGY HARSTAD CONNECTION

INVESTIGATORS THROUGHOUT the decades have attempted to establish a connection between the disappearance of Frances Ewalt and the vicious murder of Peggy Lee Harstad. On July 4, 1974, Harstad, twenty-one years of age, disappeared while driving alone from Harlowton to Rosebud. She was last seen alive around 9 p.m. that night at Melstone. By all accounts, Peggy was sweet, sincere, and painfully shy.

On July 5, 1974, her car was found within a few miles of her home, near Rosebud. On July 7, a ranch hand discovered a purse and other articles belonging to Peggy Lee in a culvert approximately ten miles west of her abandoned car. Harstad's body was found two months later in the Yellowstone River near Forsyth.

In the developing investigation, an elderly couple informed the sheriff of Rosebud County that they had seen a black man and a white man hitchhiking on the night of July 4 between Roundup and Forsyth. It was late, and there was no traffic. A car stopped. A young lady swung open the passenger door. A murder was committed.

Subsequently, two men were identified: Dewey Eugene Coleman, a black man; and Robert Dennis Nank, a white man. Nank, hoping to elude the hot jolt of the electric chair, described to investigators every minute in graphic detail.

Coleman initially was sentenced to death. Nank received a hundred-year sentence. Coleman's plea agreement dismissed the aggravated kidnapping charge, which then carried a mandatory death sentence. The 9th U.S. Circuit Court of Appeals overturned Coleman's death sentence in 1988.

Coleman died of natural causes at the Lewistown Infirmary in 2016. Nank is still serving his term. No evidence has ever been publicly or officially presented to connect Coleman and Nank to the mystery and presumed murder of Frances Ewalt.

ROBYN ANN PETTINATO

VANISHED: JULY 5, 1975
VANISHED FROM: WHITEFISH

ON THE DAY AFTER Independence Day in 1975, fourteen-year-old Robyn Ann Pettinato sucked in a few deep breaths of air full of pure heat. Her light brown, shoulder-length hair was rimmed with sweat. The days were long, and the nights short, and her attire reflected the season: cut-off jean shorts and a halter top.

It was the season for melons and baseball—in fact, a softball field radiant with activity was just a few hundred feet from her front yard—and in the West Second Street neighborhood in Whitefish people sat on their stoops in the warmth and listened to the radio. People were sunning themselves on the grass, flying kites, listening to the beats of Elton John and the Bee Gees.

Snacking on a bagel and farmer cheese, Robyn liked the swishy comfort of being barefoot. She told her mother that she was going to walk across the street to the field to watch some of the tournament and then to a friend's house, just two houses to the north of the Pettinato family home. Perhaps once she got to Kelly's house, they would play riddles and invent games and prevent the summer heat from taking over by going to the field and getting ice cream cones.

From the edge of the lawn, Robyn waved, squinting a little in the sun. Her mother waved in return.

And then Robyn simply vanished.

FIFTY YEARS OF MYSTIFICATION

ALMOST FIFTY YEARS LATER, Robyn's family and the detectives who investigated her case remain just as mystified as they were then about her disappearance.

Her diary, turned over to law enforcement officers by her older sister, Rhonda Dudis of Kalispell, gave detectives insight into her personal life and a few details to examine. There were names of crushes and boyfriends, a couple of them from the past and one that was current, and classmates who she found creepy. But they were all dead ends. The overall tone of the diary was sensible, ordinary, with little written in anger or in a mood of defiance.

"She had kept a lot of notes in her diary until the day she disappeared, and we to some extent followed her trail," said retired Whitefish detective Dan Voelker, who pursued the Pettinato case for many years. Voelker polygraphed the boyfriend, and he passed. He shook his head no and shuddered and shrugged, and at one point he even cried. Voelker didn't think that he was unforthcoming and kicked him loose.

Voelker interviewed the parents, and he found them to be genuine, sincere people who were dealing with the loss of their loved one the best they could. Voelker concluded that the Pettinatos had no idea what had happened. He regretted even once having to put them in the possible villain column, a prerequisite of the situation.

Detectives tracked down a young man Robyn referred to in her diary who had left Whitefish for another state around the time of her disappearance, but that was a dead end. Nothing in the diary suggested malevolence toward her parents or indicated that she was unhappy to the point of escape. Law enforcement officials who knew the family and knew the case went out of their way to emphasize that the Pettinatos were a "nice family" and that they never believed that anyone in the family was culpable for Robyn's loss.

Sometimes the tips were just plain preposterous—she committed suicide two blocks away; she was seen one month later drinking alone at the end of a shadowy bar; she was depressed about not having any good relationships and bought a one-way ticket to California and joined a cult; she left town with a pimp or a dealer or a married bank teller.

Sometimes tips took Montana law enforcement to far-flung locations, including Lindsborg, Kansas, and a small town in Oklahoma. But they could find nothing to indicate that Robyn was the person in question. Voelker also checked Social Security and Internal Revenue Service records through the years to see if Robyn's name came up. Nothing ever surfaced.

Early speculation was that Robyn may have run away from home, but Voelker and Robyn's family members agreed that theory didn't make much sense because she had left her purse behind and didn't even have on shoes.

SISTER KEEPS SEARCHING

Born November 12, 1960, Robyn was eight years younger than Rhonda. Age twenty-three when her sister vanished, Rhonda said that she had found it difficult to relate to and connect with her fourteen-year-old sibling. They weren't necessarily tightly bonded. Her kid sister was "a talkative little pest" and "the typical little pain in the neck" for a long time. Then Rhonda went away to college in Bozeman.

But Rhonda returned to the Flathead Valley in June 1975 because she had been offered a teaching job at Flathead High

School. Robyn was excited that her older sister was going to be close to home, and their relationship strengthened.

Through the years Rhonda, one of five Pettinato siblings, became the primary family contact who worked with detectives and the press. When she spoke, she spoke on behalf of them all. She was the one who provided a snippet of her own hair that continues to be a DNA sample on file. She also was involved when a spiritual medium was hired in the early 1980s to help with the case. (The medium, she said, turned out to be more trouble than truth finder.)

"My parents were both destroyed by what happened," she said. "What could alleviate that kind of pain? Mom couldn't handle it; Dad shut off."

Robyn's father, Romolo Pettinato, was born in Whitefish in 1924, and in May 1943 he was drafted into the U.S. Army, where he was assigned to the 13th Engineer Battalion Company C. He served in World War II in the Pacific Theater. During his training in Wyoming, he met Esther Schwartzkopf, and they were married in 1945.

After being discharged in 1946, Romolo and Esther settled in Essex, where he was employed by the Great Northern Railroad as a machinist. Romolo became a locomotive fireman and brakeman and moved his family to Whitefish in 1960. Romolo continued his career with the railroad until retiring in 1988. Romolo died in September 1998, only a few months after Esther. In addition to Rhonda, Robyn has two brothers and another sister, but Rhonda has been the visible flame keeping the search aglow.

Rhonda harbors no ill will toward the investigators who worked her sister's case over the years. It was the hurtful, false allegations of some neighbors, the ones who stoked the small-town gossip mill and churned out ugly rumors, that caused her to hold certain people in low regard. It's a uniquely painful experience to be victimized twice, once by an unknown perpetrator and once more by the malicious gossip in the community.

"Dad was gentle, and he would never have hurt or done something like that to one of his children," Rhonda said. "Why? It isn't something that is even fathomable to me. She had a family who loved her."

Rhonda also pointed out that her father had just gotten back from his shift as a brakeman for the railroad when he learned that his daughter was missing. He had an ironclad alibi—a punch card, coworkers, a train schedule and itinerary.

ASSUMED AS A RUNAWAY; PERCEIVED LACK OF EMERGENCY, SAID SISTER

THE MID-1970S "were a different period and a different place when it came to missing kids," Rhonda said. "Back then police wrote you off as a runaway, like you zipped off on your own, until something proved otherwise."

In Rhonda's opinion, the investigation was marked by what she considered to be a lack of urgency and a lack of emergency. Indeed, there was no Amber Alert system for missing children in 1975, and such cases were often informed by a lackadaisical wait-and-see approach from local law enforcement.

Perhaps Rhonda is correct when she points out that most of the media in her sister's case seemed to have dismissed hers as the tale of an unfortunate, troubled runaway. Local newspapers didn't follow the missing person case to any significant degree. For example, the front page of the July 31, 1975, edition of the *Whitefish Pilot* held a short report about Robyn Pettinato, noting that she had disappeared on July 5 and was "presumed to be a runaway" and had not been heard from since. Later that summer a quarter-page advertisement was published in the *Whitefish Pilot*, showing Robyn's photo and listing her essential physical statistics—five feet tall, one hundred pounds, blue eyes—and offering a $50 reward.

A six-paragraph update in the *Daily Inter Lake* in early September said the police had checked various leads but quoted a resigned Whitefish police chief, Jim Loser, as saying, "unfortunately, there's nothing we can do to pin it down and tell you more." Loser said he hoped that the case would be solved before long and that it was "very, very frustrating" to not have any of the most basic answers.

TED BUNDY CONNECTION THEORIZED

SOMETIME IN THE LATE 1980s, Voelker fielded a phone call from federal agents who said the Whitefish teen matched the profile of the victims of serial killer Ted Bundy, who was executed in Florida's electric chair in 1989.

Put to death for the kidnapping and murder of a twelve-year-old girl, Bundy, in a spate of eleventh-hour confessions, claimed to have killed as many as fifty young women in Utah, Washington, Idaho, Colorado, and Florida from 1973 to 1978.

In June 1975, Bundy captured and killed Susan Curtis, fifteen, when she was attending the Bountiful Orchard Youth Conference at Brigham Young University in Utah. Bundy claimed he buried her body near a highway, but her remains have never been located.

On August 16, 1975, at 2:30 a.m., Bundy was arrested for the first time in Granger, Utah, after a chase by the Utah highway patrol. Police found disguises, gloves, rope, duct tape, a crowbar, and several sets of handcuffs in his car. He was released on bail the next day. Using all the available information present at the time, Detective Voelker and his partners could not document that Bundy was ever in Montana.

One of the investigators who reexamined the case in 1985 said that everything related to the Pettinato case was contained in a shoebox at the Whitefish Police Department and he noted that there hadn't been any activity on her Social Security number.

Every few years a new investigator re-examined and delved back into the case, but to no avail.

In 1996, Esther Pettinato told the television show *A Current Affair* that "absolutely nothing" had happened in the twenty years since her daughter vanished to shed any light on the case. She conceded that she had virtually given up on the possibility of ever learning the details of what happened to Robyn. After so long with zero leads, she said she could only assume the most horrible—that she'd never see her daughter again. "You always keep hope alive," said Esther. "But, after all these years, you just kind of give up."

Less than a year after Robyn went missing, another teen girl, Nancy Kirkpatrick, disappeared from a town about ten miles from Whitefish. She has never been found. One theory is that there is some correlation between the two vanishings, but this hasn't been proved.

NANCY LYNN KIRKPATRICK

VANISHED: APRIL 21, 1976
VANISHED FROM: COLUMBIA FALLS

NANCY KIRKPATRICK was a typical sixteen-year-old girl—she fantasized about travel and having money, and she loved art and painting and spending time with her friends. And similar to many other sixteen-year-olds, she had a hard time just trying to make it to tomorrow. Her life felt as if it were on an inevitable collision course with her family. Her father was a mean-spirited domestic tyrant, and her mother was at one time committed to a state institution for debilitating mental health issues. People who knew Nancy's family summed up the essence of her family life in one word: "broken."

In many ways, she was the "normal" teenager that loved ones cherished: she received good grades, loved to be hiking or camping or rafting, loved the bounty of the Flathead Valley cherries in the summer. But also a dark thread ran in her. She was obsessed with the hippie counterculture and showed a perverse interest in old *Life* magazine articles about Charles Manson. She talked freely and cussedly about sex and spoke of "the free love" that she'd read of and was told about as a philosophical state of mind. She talked often about escaping to the anonymity of the city, the West Coast, where she could experiment with whatever and whoever she wanted. She told one of her school counselors that she had dreams about

Sixteen-year-old Nancy Kirkpatrick of Columbia Falls vanished in April 1976. Nancy, a habitual runaway, babysat for a neighborhood family that evening and she was last seen walking home afterward. The distance between the two residences was approximately one mile. Relatives and police thought Nancy had run away again. But this time, the teen never resurfaced. This extended absence led authorities to switch their mode of examination and suspect foul play.
COURTESY FLATHEAD COUNTY SHERIFF'S OFFICE/PUBLIC DOMAIN

tombstones all over the place and tripping over them in her garden and backyard.

Nancy's problems seem to get worse after her parents divorced, and she was sent to live with her grandmother in Columbia Falls. Her grandmother was sweet and kind, but she was overwhelmed by the kid's emotional turmoil.

She was a habitual runaway and had traveled as far as Seattle and Los Angeles. She had that peculiar self-assurance of the very young—in her case, the simple presumption that she could get away when she needed, anytime she wanted, and that in so doing that she could outrun her troubles. Sometimes she would take off with an older friend. At least twice, she journeyed alone. She would sleep in bus stations and terminals and liked the feeling of being barely visible, camouflaged. Sometimes she would crash at an apartment of a stranger with a sofa bed. In downtown Los Angeles, she talked nonstop with the taxi driver who took her down dangerously close to the Skid Row area. She bantered with the drug dealers and hippie drifters in Hollywood, high fiving someone who'd offered her a nickel bag. She saw and heard the humming of the drug-induced Hare Krishnas, a peculiar form of Hinduism founded on the opposite coast a decade earlier. It was a long way from the mountains of western Montana.

To her grandmother's relief, the police in those states would always find her, and someone in a uniform would eventually bring her home. She would bolt. She would be retrieved. She'd return to her grandmother's.

Her grandmother assumed that one day she would attempt to flee again, that she wouldn't arrive home as expected. It was also assumed that she would be returned—and that eventually she would snap out of it, outgrow the rebellion and defiance, and outgrow all the jittery teenage angst. It was assumed that she would live to be an adult, a wise, ripened adult who one day would look back in hindsight on all the mischief and naivete that marked her youth with fond, proud bliss.

But that's evidently not the case for her.

PRESUMED THAT SHE RAN AWAY AGAIN

IT WAS APRIL 21, 1976. Nancy Fitzpatrick began the morning in lockup in Kalispell, Montana, after the police in Seattle returned her to Montana. A few days earlier, she had been found in a supermarket parking lot and told a Seattle police officer on patrol she had no money and had been hitchhiking. He leaned back, shaking his head. He fired off a long list of bad things that could have happened to her. But she was safe—at least, for now. Kalispell police had the girl transported to Spokane, where they had picked her up the previous afternoon. She was released shortly after noon on her grandmother's recognizance, and the two of them returned to Columbia Falls.

Nancy babysat for a neighborhood family that evening, and she was last seen walking home afterward. The distance between the two residences was approximately one mile.

Relatives and police thought Nancy had run away again. But this time, the teen never resurfaced. This extended absence led authorities to switch their mode of examination and suspect foul play.

Retired Whitefish Police Detective Dan Voelker never minced words when he described the pessimism that he felt that dogged him while he was investigating Nancy's disappearance. "We had not a single clue," said Voelker. "It was brutal. We had nothing. Your mind runs in a thousand directions." Voelker inherited the case four years after the fact in 1980, epochs and epochs of lost time in cold case years.

The trail was icy until May 1983, when a grade-school teacher of Kirkpatrick's claimed to have spotted her in the Frontier Bar in Anchorage, Alaska. In the dark, oaky bar, he noticed a girl who looked identical to Kirkpatrick fidgeting at the phone booth in the corner. She had her hair pulled in a tight bun, wore a loose blue dress, and didn't look very well-groomed or collected. She said that she was from a little town near Glacier National Park and indicated that she was interested in not being located.

Voelker said that he interviewed the teacher extensively and Alaska State Police investigated, including a check of the bar and a roundup of its patrons, but "we could never come up with anything." Since then, very little has been written or reported of note about the status of the Kirkpatrick disappearance. There has been no massive media frenzy or much publicized exposure, primarily because the one who perhaps loved Nancy the dearest—her grandmother—is long deceased.

PETTINATO-KIRKPATRICK POSSIBLE CONNECTION

LESS THAN A YEAR before Nancy went missing, another teen girl, Robyn Pettinato, fourteen, disappeared from a town not far from Columbia Falls. She, too, has never been found.

Pat Walsh, a retired sergeant with the Flathead County Sheriff's Office, said in 2023 that he continues to believe the disappearance of Robyn Pettinato from Whitefish on July 5, 1975, somehow connects to vanishing Nancy Kirkpatrick's. For decades he has exasperatingly tried—and failed—to link the two.

"There are commonalities beyond mere coincidences lurking there," Walsh said.

MARSHA HELGESON

MURDERED: SEPTEMBER 9, 1978
MURDER LOCATION: BILLINGS

SHE HAD REDDISH-COLORED HAIR, and she projected a charming but troubled presence. The people who knew and loved her said she was very radiant, friendly, talkative, a lover of coffee and book discussion groups. But she had a wilder side, a maddeningly contradictory rebelliousness.

At the diner in Billings where she ate her final meal, patrons described seeing "a pleasant-looking woman," clad in blue jeans and a white top with yellow embroidery, and a silver choker with gold birds. One of them even remembered her blue fingernail polish. Another recalled that she glanced at him and smiled.

DISCOVERED NAKED IN THE WEEDS

THE COLD CASE of twenty-one-year-old Marsha Lynn Helgeson marked its forty-fifth anniversary. Case number 78-72460 opened on September 9, 1978, when Helgeson's partially nude body was found on Alkali Creek Road in Billings Heights. The autopsy of Marsha's body revealed that she was stabbed several times and had noticeable lacerations on her face. The red welts on the cheeks and jaw and neck resembled burns from a hot pad. A homeowner, Donald Nave,

The cold case of twenty-one-year-old Marsha Lynn Helgeson marked its forty-fifth anniversary. Case number 78-72460 opened on September 9, 1978, when Helgeson's partially nude body was found on Alkali Creek Road in Billings Heights. The autopsy report said that she died of "multiple stab wounds," and she had noticeable lacerations on her face.
COURTESY PAT EAKINS

from 2139 Alkali Creek Road discovered Helgeson's body in the weeds at the edge of the driveway in the morning hours.

At the time of the murder, Helgeson lived alone at 2014 Dickie Road in Billings. An investigation of Helgeson found that she was comfortable roaming the streets at night alone or with friends. And it seems as if that was what she did on her final night. At about midnight, Helgeson wandered around the night structure of the city, among the solidity of the dark buildings, and among the colors of traffic lights reflected in the shining black street. Couples strolled in and out of the streetlights. Downtown was thwacking with an odd mix of hardened, heavy-drinking locals, toughs from nearby Hardin, many of them with unfriendly intentions—a palpable enmity could be felt in the air between reservation and city kids in Billings in the late 1970s—and a smattering of tourists.

LAST MEAL AT SAMBO'S

SOMETIME BETWEEN 1:15 and 2 a.m., Marsha sat at a booth and ate a salad and a few french fries at Sambo's restaurant on 24th Street West. She had been at the 17 Bar earlier, and the food offered a much-needed respite from the alcohol. Sambo's had a reputation for low-quality, high-volume food service. People ate there late, and some ate there often, especially those who were less concerned with the quality of a fancy meal and more focused on not running up too much debt.

Several witnesses provided similarly consistent descriptions of Helgeson to the Yellowstone County Sheriff's Office: approximately 105 pounds; five feet, three inches tall; reddish-blonde hair, shoulder length; Levis and a white top with flower trim.

She was not alone at the eatery. She sat with a man or woman who has never been identified, and Billings authorities believed that the person with Helgeson was the crucial bridge that they needed to cross to solve the crime. Officers obtained a rough description, but the sketch that came out of it was comically inept. For starters, detectives working on the case couldn't identify the suspect as a man or a woman.

Detectives searched for two young men who were seen talking to Helgeson in the restaurant that night. Police at first said the two were "not suspects" in the case but perhaps would be able to provide a description of the victim's companion.

All the witnesses furnished the police with descriptions of these two male strangers. All of them wished they had taken more notice at the time, but how were they to know they would need to? Detectives plastered downtown Billings with posters: they wanted to talk to anyone who may have been in Sambo's that morning between 1:15 and 2 a.m.

Officers looked through the restaurant's customer checks and found Marsha's order for salad, a root beer, and french fries. An autopsy report confirmed that that was what she had eaten just before her death. The mysterious companion must not have ordered a meal or ordered on a separate ticket. Perhaps the accompanying person accosted the young woman, alone, attractive, for the purpose of some type of criminal procurement, police theorized.

Reports are conflicting as to what happened next. Some news accounts at the time stated that she and the unidentified person left Sambo's together, and at least two of them said that "she left with the two young men." One of the police detectives who reexamined the case several years ago repeated the latter claim, asserting that Helgeson and the two men together seemed to have even returned to the 17 Bar.

SATURDAY MORNING DISCOVERY OF VICTIM

SOMETHING VICIOUS AND EVIL transpired between the time that Helgeson consumed her early morning meal and the time that her nude body, with "multiple stab wounds," was found about 9:30 Saturday morning near Alkali Creek Road.

What is known is that Donald Nave called the sheriff's office and reported that a woman's body had been found north of Billings Logan International Airport, alongside the gravel road, about two miles from the city limits. Nave and one of his unidentified relatives discovered her. By the time police arrived, so had a number of gawkers. There were injuries to the woman's face, one witness told the newspapers. There are pools of strawberry- and rhubarb-colored bloodstains from head to toe, another said.

Uniformed cops and detectives in plain clothes were coming and going in every direction. Red-siren patrol cars were scattered thickly, and a pair of ambulances threaded through the maze. Deputies blocked off the area, made plaster casts of tracks, and examined the scene. Officers collected clothing in the brush and secured clues through the afternoon. Then the body was bagged and removed and flown by charter aircraft to Great Falls, where Dr. John Pfaff, pathologist, performed an autopsy.

Pfaff noted that her torso sustained numerous stab abrasions, and there were "other signs of violence on the body besides the stab wounds," Pfaff wrote.

That evening one of the investigators told a Billings radio program that the young woman was "probably killed at the scene" where her body was found, and that deputies found a knife that "may be the murder weapon."

SOCIAL AUTOPSY OF HELGESON

BORN MAY 29, 1957, in Billings, Marsha Helgeson came into the world with plenty of love and support. Her parents, Berton and Helen, married in 1953; from this marriage, five children were born. Helen loved to take the kids fishing, one of her favorite pastimes. Marsha was by all accounts an easy child to be around—one who could keep herself occupied drawing, reading, and writing in her journals. Marsha graduated from the long, waxy halls of Billings Senior High School in 1974. She loved her classes and the field trips, and she joined a few clubs—chess, reading, debate, speech—and she even more loved the summers and how the days stretched on forever. There were the usual rites of passage—awkward dating, sweaty palms and proms and corsages and making out in cars. It was a cliquey place. She created her own. She had a few minor skirmishes with the law—open containers, warnings about trespassing—but she was always quiet and cooperative with the authorities.

At twenty-one years old, Helgeson was single, working at Degel's Dairy Queen, 4242 State, as a cook. It was a decent living, she told friends, but somewhere along the line it might be wise to move to a bigger town, perhaps Denver. She had recently purchased a clunker from the rows of cars for sale on an east side used car lot, and sometimes she would drive on the highway, the nose of the vehicle pointing south, and she would think about just what the wider world might have in store. Sometimes she talked about how life just didn't "seem to amount to much." She talked about how hard it was to picture herself growing old in Billings, or even staying as long as she had stayed, and she was beginning to think that she had stayed too long. Still, she kept her attitude lighthearted.

Nick Degel, owner, said she had worked for him about three weeks. "She was a nice girl to get along with and easy going," Degel told the Associated Press. "She did her work here, and she was pleasant." She worked until about 5 p.m. Friday, picked up her week's paycheck for about $90, and left, apparently by herself, Degel said. "That's the last I saw her. Next time was in the papers."

CLUES, REWARDS, AND GUESSES

THE SHERIFF'S DEPARTMENT said that on the evening of her murder she was home with her sister until about 8:30 p.m. That's about the time Marsha said she was going out for a drive and hopped into her sister's car; her own vehicle had a badly cracked windshield, which she had an upcoming appointment to fix. She didn't say if she was going to meet a friend, but she did mention "checking out the music" or possibly stopping at a local bar to have a drink or two.

Information on her whereabouts—who she was with, where she was, and for how long—after she left her sister— has always been a matter of conjecture. Operating on the margins of society, Marsha left only hints and inklings. In fact, the authorities said that they had a hard time even finding a recent photo of her. None appeared in high school yearbooks after her sophomore year.

The car that Marsha borrowed from her sister was found, and police speculated that she had been forced or pulled from it; it was solidly linked to the crime. Police refused to specify where the vehicle was found. The young woman was believed to have been taken to the murder scene in another vehicle— never publicly identified or located. Sheriff's officers collected shredded, bloodstained clothing at the scene and speculated that the murder was "sexually related," saying that her "clothes had been torn away," but never elaborated on whether she had been raped. The approximate time of her death was not specified in the pathologist's report.

A few months after the murder, Crime Stoppers offered a reward of $1,000 to help break the case, asking the public to help identify the two male "persons of interest" last seen with Marsha. The Crime Stoppers account said that Marsha was "last seen at the 17 Bar with two similarly aged men at 1 o'clock that morning" and made no reference to Sambo's or the other mysterious composite.

One man was described as in his early twenties; six feet tall, of slender build; with stringy, brown hair, cut short; wearing jeans, a Western-style shirt, and boots. The other man was described as about twenty-five years old; about five feet, nine

inches tall; and 160 pounds, of muscular build; high cheek-
bones and straight, brown hair that covered his ears; wearing
jeans, a Western-style shirt, and boots.

RISKY LIFESTYLE MAY HAVE LED
TO VICTIMIZATION

DETECTIVE SHANE BANCROFT of the Yellowstone County
Sheriff's Office said in 2023 that Helgeson was not a prostitute, but elements of her life put her at risk for being murdered. "She had a variety of friends who she was comfortable
on the street running around with," said Bancroft. "She was
the type of person who would run off with a variety of people
on any given day. She had a free lifestyle and came and went
freely. She was comfortable on the streets."

One other item of interest: the band Boston played in
Billings on the night of the murder—a big event drawing
plenty of strangers to the city. Investigators reexamining the
case, including Bancroft, wondered if there was a connection
between the concert and Helgeson's death, unsure if she was
even there or if she had friends at the concert.

"We certainly know that people from her circle had come
and gone from the concert," said Bancroft. "Could it be something of significance?"

POSSIBLE LINKS TO OTHER CRIMES

LARRY LYLE COX, thirty, Billings theater manager, was stabbed
to death near Columbus a few days before Helgeson. A sketch
artist depicted the alleged culprit as a haggard-looking black
man with an oversize Renaissance-style hat. Police said that

they saw no connection between the two murders, but that they couldn't "discredit it entirely" either. An arrest was eventually made in the slaying.

On January 10, 1979, thirty-three-year-old Charlene Victoria Cumings was murdered in the early morning hours in Everett, Washington. Her nude body was found by two railroad men in an open field at a construction site. She had been choked and stabbed repeatedly. Montana police said that the Washington murder and the Helgeson murder shared similarities that were too striking to dismiss the possibility. Detectives in Billings refused to state publicly what those similarities were. No arrests were ever made in the murder of Cumings.

Marsha's murder was eerily similar to another horrific incident that took place in Billings on August 30, 1979, when a nineteen-year-old Billings woman was abducted from a downtown street, raped, choked, and nearly drowned. The woman swam away from her assailant in the Yellowstone River. Billings police detectives told the media that the attack had strong similarities to the murder of Marsha Helgeson, but they declined to explain them. The woman was reportedly abducted about 8:30 p.m. from a downtown location while she was with a girlfriend and then taken to an area on the Yellowstone River.

Authorities said the woman was sexually assaulted. Her assailant, described by sources only as a "nonwhite male," first attempted to strangle her and then tried to drown her. She escaped by swimming across the river. Police officers theorized that her abductor probably thought he had killed her.

Police searched for the driver of a yellow Pontiac Trans Am with Big Horn County license plates in connection with the crime. But no arrest was ever made.

Sadly, no new information or material about the Helgeson murder appears in even a single newspaper article after 1980.

Marsha's father, Berton, died in 1981. Her mother, Helen, died in 2004.

RUTH LORI BALLEW

OVER THE YEARS, investigators attempted to establish a link between Helgeson's murder and the killing of Ruth Lori Ballew, a twenty-one-year-old woman who died of multiple gunshot and stab wounds following an assault on February 5, 1977. Ballew was found on a road leading to the city dump. But unlike Helgeson, Ballew had a well-documented history of social and criminal problems, including a record of prostitution arrests.

COLD CASE UNIT FOR
YELLOWSTONE COUNTY

EVIDENCE COLLECTED at the time of Helgeson's murder in 1978 that had little to no usefulness at the time is of immense value now for investigators. Perhaps the exotic mystery of DNA analysis will ultimately reveal what years of monotonous police work could not.

Around 2010, the Yellowstone County Sheriff's Office established the Cold Case Unit for the county to review unsolved homicide cases dating back to the early 1970s. The murder of Marsha Helgeson is one of them.

"Investigators at the time did an outstanding scene investigation," said Bancroft. "They collected all kinds of minutiae, and it is stuff that we are still processing today."

Anyone with information regarding the murder of Marsha Helgeson may contact the Yellowstone County Sheriff's Office Cold Case Unit at (406) 869-3530.

CORINA CONTRERAZ

MURDERED: DECEMBER 22, 1978
MURDER LOCATION: BILLINGS

A SHORT WALK HOME at an imprudent hour cost a Billings teenager her life. And, sadly, that is about the entire extent of what we know about her and her short existence. We know who died and how. Perhaps we will never know why or by whom.

Some homicide cases seem to be covered ad infinitum and some yield a treasure trove of documents, interviews, police reports, and people connected to the investigation who are willing to keep stories in the public consciousness. Other cases yield stubbornly little, not a single substantive article about the victim or their circumstances. Corina Lydia Contreraz, alas, falls into the latter category. Some newspaper snippets—and the word "fragment" would be a generous description of the four to six sentences that she usually received—even failed to correctly identify her age.

Contreraz was sixteen years of age—not seventeen as some newspaper and online sources state—when she was found brutally beaten, stabbed, and strangled on the morning of Friday, December 22, 1978.

"A very violent, violent crime," according to one officer intimately familiar with the case. "It was purely vicious."

Her partially clothed body was found at the Pryor Creek interchange of Interstate 90, about eleven miles east of Billings. Instead of dumping the body somewhere among the millions of acres of rural, rugged Montana, the body was in essence ditched in an open and visible driveway. Corina's body was discovered by a Worden school-bus driver, Clyde Fleming, who was making his outbound run before daylight. It lay in a grotesque position on its stomach at a right angle to the mailbox, one arm outflung, the other beneath the body. The side of the face turned up had been battered beyond recognition.

END OF A LIFE

SHE SPENT HER FINAL NIGHT at a friend's house and was last seen walking from there at about 3 a.m., presumably to her own residence. Something new was in the air, just starting out: winter. In fact, the temperature hovered in single digits for most of the early morning. Thousands of pale stars swirled over Corina's head.

The distance between the two houses—Corina's friend's and her own—is not mentioned in the stubbornly scant police reports. According to her friend, Corina had been smoking marijuana and she was tree-top high. She was dressed in light, loose clothing and wasn't wearing a coat.

"That was not uncommon for her, despite her young age," said Detective Shane Bancroft of the Yellowstone County Sheriff's Office. "She was very comfortable leaving her house at three o'clock to visit friends or to hang out with a boyfriend or other friends. She lived in a close-knit community where she would pass back and forth between family and friends' homes easily. Not uncommon for her father not to know where she was. Her dad didn't know where she was and not in a neglectful way. She had a lot of freedom. She was 16 years old in 1978 and she had the freedom to be in the Billings community on her own."

TOO MANY UNKNOWNS, BLANK SPACES

IN THE TYPICAL homicide investigation, the police turn the life of the victim into a file of records, information, dates, times, places, and people so that in the end there are no blank spaces, no mysteries, no unknowns, and no privacy. In Corina's case it seems the opposite happened: it's all blank spaces and unknowns and mysteries. Recently, one of her older brothers said that he knew almost nothing about the incident, even the basics, and that he had never once been questioned about his sister by authorities. A records request about Corina yielded just a single, half-page document from the files of the Cold Case Unit for Yellowstone County. There is something depressingly bleak and insufficient about the available written record of the teenager's existence.

It was reported at the time that she may have been hitch-hiking to visit a boyfriend in Pryor, but Bancroft said that Corina's friends even to this day do not recall her mentioning such a thing that night.

"Possible," said Bancroft. "But friends who knew her said it never came up."

Bancroft said that he believes that Corina knew her killer.

"I can't imagine someone, anyone getting into a car with a complete stranger without having some level of comfort," said Bancroft. "But it's hard to say because of her lifestyle."

As far as suspects, Bancroft said that all the signs and arrows pointed to the probability that it was someone who knew the victim and lived within close proximity to her. He said that the boyfriend was questioned and released.

"There was some evidence that tied back to the neighbor-hood that she lived in," said Bancroft.

Corina was born in Cleveland, Ohio, and she attended Little Flower Elementary School and later Riverside Junior High School. She was a member of the youth club at Our Lady of Guadalupe Catholic parish. Her parents, Ray and Jennie Contreraz, had moved to Billings from the Midwest in the early 1960s. According to family members, Corina attended school only sporadically. She went for weeks or sometimes months at a time, then abruptly stopped showing up. Other pupils were far ahead of her. They had passed her by, and no teacher ever took the trouble to discover the fundamental gap in her education, still less to remedy it. Bewildered, bored, apathetic, she sat at the back of the classroom, staring at the incomprehensible on page or blackboard.

Tragedy seemed to plague the Contreraz family. Her mother died of an aggressive form of cancer in September 1974; and her sister, Sharon Contreraz, was killed in an automobile accident in November 1976, plowed down by a drunken motorist while walking to the grocers.

MURDER OF "QUIET DROPOUT"

AT THE TIME OF THE MURDER, Corina lived with her father at 623 S. 34th in Billings, and the building was teeming to overflowing with his many children: Corina lived with three brothers and three sisters, and Ray also had at least three other children subsequent to Jennie's death. To the east, there wasn't much to look at, just a deserted jungle of warehouses and junkyards. It was a red stone building with granite trim around the windows and along the roofline; it had a grand curving double front stoop. Flocks of kids sat and sprawled all up and down both sets of stairs and clustered on the stone steps or hung on the railings. Passersby could have assumed that it was a school. It had no land in the back. The building was later converted into a three-floor apartment house. As dusk settled, Corina would ignore the smaller children, seeking the darker, even illicit possibilities of her teenage temptations, truant friends, cheap alcohol from the unscrupulous distributors who sold to minors, approval of the opposite sex, recreational drugs. She would say good-bye to the younger ones, suck in the evening air, and disappear into the darkness.

Corina was a "quiet dropout," according to law enforcement, and at the time of her murder she would have—and should have—been a sophomore at Billings Senior High School. Though it had been inferred, Bancroft said he found no evidence to believe that she was working as a prostitute.

LINK TO HELGESON MURDER POSSIBLE

DETECTIVE BANCROFT SAID that he had a hard time dismissing the idea that the murder of Corina was connected to the murder of Marsha Helgeson in September 1978.

"The coincidences are much too hard to ignore," said Bancroft. "Looking at the two crime scenes, the location of where the bodies were found, the ages and lifestyles of the victims, and the same manner of death, I find it hard to believe that they are not connected. They can't be overlooked."

Corina was buried at Holy Cross Cemetery, in the suburbs of Cleveland.

Anyone with information regarding the murder of Corina Lynn Contreraz may contact the Yellowstone County Sheriff's Office Cold Case Unit at (406) 869-3530.

PEGGY JO DECOTEAU

VANISHED: JULY 4, 1979
VANISHED FROM: SUPERIOR

PEGGY DECOTEAU and her husband, Earl, had traveled from their home in Maple Valley, Washington, to visit relatives in North Dakota, and they stopped at the Big Sky Motel in Superior on the return leg. The vacation hadn't gone so well for either of them so far. At five feet, four inches tall but weighing more than 155 pounds, Peggy wasn't one to be physically intimidated by her husband. They'd fought most of the time, and neither of them held back on the name-calling. The fighting was solid, steady, and there was no getting away from it. Perhaps the ride back home seemed like an eternity to Peggy and to Earl, too.

On July 4, 1979, Earl said he woke up in their room at 11 p.m. Peggy was gone. He stepped outside. It was drizzling slightly. The parking lot was lit and shone with rain. The vehicle remained in the same location that it had been when Earl had parked it earlier in the evening. He went inside and went back to sleep.

According to his police statement, he said that the couple had arrived at the motel at about 6 p.m., and both had promptly fallen asleep. He had felt dehydrated after the long drive and walked into the bathroom, ran cold water in a plastic cup, and finished the soft drink that was in the small, convenience refrigerator. The room had two beds, and nobody was in the other bed when he woke up before midnight.

She has not been seen since.

"SERIOUS MARITAL PROBLEMS" CITED

AT FIRST, Earl did not report Peggy missing or report the disappearance to the police; in the meantime, he said he tried to find Peggy by checking to see if she was with various friends and relatives. It was no secret that the DeCoteaus had been having "serious marital problems," according to published press releases, and investigators believed at first that because Peggy's purse, credit cards, and travel bag were missing, she had left of her own accord. Peggy's credit cards were never used.

The physical description of the forty-year-old woman was generically fuzzy: "short, light auburn hair, blue eyes, a mole on the right side of her face." Peggy was said to be wearing Levis jeans, carrying a light denim travel bag, as well as a brown leather purse, which contained approximately $200 in cash.

Barbara Maldonado, DeCoteaus' daughter, reported July 13 to the sheriff's office that her mother had disappeared from the motel. She explained that she and her father waited more than a week to report the incident because they were checking with friends and relatives. Mineral County Undersheriff and Coroner Anita Parkin said that she and other police officers canvassed the area expecting to find the woman's corpse. "We've investigated several grave sites that we thought may have been hers, but nothing has shown up," Parkin said that summer.

Peggy's credit cards were never used, and her Social Security number has remained dormant of action. Peggy's death

is officially classified by the Mineral County Sheriff's department as an unsolved murder. But it doesn't appear as if anyone has made much of an effort over the years to rescue the
case from irrelevance.

"We don't even look at it anymore," said Pat Hines, spokesperson for the Mineral County Sheriff's Office. "It'd be great
to find the body. But, you know, Earl is about ninety years old
and living in North Dakota, and we just couldn't do much
about it."

Most of the paperwork related to the case, including Earl's
three-page statement, recorded almost ten days after the disappearance, has been heavily redacted. The paper-thin case
file contains little but the basic time line and short interviews
with Peggy's husband and family. Notations on one of the
pages perhaps indicate the most honest interpretation of the
diagnosis and prognosis of the case. "Husband said she was
gone." "Husband can't be detained." "No body." "Most likely
husband involved."

JUDY FOCHER

VANISHED: MAY 24, 1980
VANISHED FROM: DILLON
FOUND MURDERED: JUNE 21, 1980

THE LATE MAY SUNSET was a winter sunset, sharp-edged and bright, colors holding their own, blue and white not melting together. It was a typical day at the laundry business—long, noisy, and familiar. Judy Focher, thirty-seven, didn't mind the slow character of the work. She and her husband, Norm, rotated and balanced all the responsibilities; and she broke up the routine listening to her Walkman or reading or talking with patrons or visitors. And there was never a shortage of visitors to see Judy.

"She was the most beautiful woman in Dillon," one person who knew her related all these years later. "She stood out for her beauty."

Saturday, May 24, 1980. Judy stared at the sunlight on the wall, which was late afternoon sunlight, getting more golden by the minute. She telephoned her husband, and they talked about the day and their plans for the summer. Invigorating plans always restored her. So, too, did hikes. And fresh air. She wandered around the outside of the building and soaked it all in; the cold air made her feel younger, and it revived her, too. There'd been a shower. The parking lot was wet.

Customers floated in and out of the laundry business into the evening. Judy and Norm didn't always keep standard hours.

If someone arrived just at the moment they were locking up, they'd flip the lights back on and stick around for another cycle of washing and drying. In some ways, it provided an essential community service—and it was profitable enough.

The Fochers were married for eighteen years. The couple met in Alaska. Norm, a native of Billings, was working as a mailman in Anchorage. Born in Grafton, North Dakota, Judy also had family living in Montana. The coincidence was their initial bond. They had two children together. Neither of them had any gripes with their position in life—at least, not publicly. Rumors circulated from those who were close to Judy who said that their marriage was hanging together by a thread. But what marriage isn't tested to its nucleus?

At 9 p.m. a regular customer came in to wash a set of bedsheets, and two kids from the local college brought in two sacks of laundry apiece. At about 10 p.m. Judy telephoned Norm again. She had just finished cleaning some of the machines and adjusting one especially temperamental coin slot. She would be leaving in just a few minutes and be home soon.

One hour later, Norm Focher hopped into his vehicle and drove to the laundromat. All the doors were unlocked. All the lights were still turned on. He walked over to Judy's battered little black sedan, which was parked outside. The interior lights were on. But there was no sign of a struggle—nothing for the lab boys to bag, wrap, and analyze. He returned to the building, where he found the day's receipts—approximately $1,000, mostly in single bills—lying on her desk, next to her purse and car and business keys.

Hit with a sudden pang of loss and fear, Norman immediately called the police and notified them that something was terribly amiss. Norman stayed up through Sunday morning before crashing from exhaustion.

INVESTIGATION STARTS

THE WORK HAD BEGUN. The investigation was underway, and everyone was mystified. The police confiscated her address book and her pile of letters. They had snapshots and notebooks. They knew where she worked and where she lived and where she came from, but they had the hardest part left to do. They had to find her life and discover her habits.

From the start, Norman Focher believed that his wife had been forcibly abducted. Meanwhile, Beaverhead County officials continued to investigate all possibilities and, naturally, Norm was considered one of them. Perhaps she was fleeing an unhappy marriage. Perhaps she suffered an inexplicable medical issue. They rattled off the list of possibilities. Norman was under suspicion, and he hated the insinuation. He told people that he believed a couple of local men had abducted her. He even turned to psychics for help in locating her.

SUICIDE OF MAIN SUSPECT DECLARED

IN THE SUBSEQUENT WEEKS, a Dillon man, who was questioned twice about the woman's disappearance, allegedly killed himself a few hours after the second interrogation, according to Beaverhead County Sheriff Buzz Davis.

Identified by Davis as the "main suspect," Bill James, thirty-eight, was found on a Sunday afternoon asphyxiated in his 1988 Dodge Shelby Dakota near Argenta, about fifteen miles west of Dillon.

The coroner told the media that a preliminary autopsy indicated he died of carbon monoxide poisoning. The sheriff said he "had been playing cat and mouse" with James about

Focher's disappearance. James was first interviewed on May 30 and once again one week later, but according to published news accounts, "denied any knowledge of the woman on both occasions," according to the sheriff. Davis clarified that he did "not know how well," or even if, James and Judy Focher were acquainted.

Davis said James worked for a bar supply and had filled the soft drink machine in the Fochers' laundry on quite a few occasions. A search party was prompted "after two notes were found in James's home," according to one published account. One was addressed to his wife, the other to Undersheriff Rick Later. Could the notes have been confessions? Davis did not disclose the contents of the notes, and just what was written in these messages has been lost to history, not included in the available documents. Papers provided after a records inquiry failed to yield a single detail about the subject matter of the alleged "notes."

Davis declared that he was "reasonably sure" Focher also was dead, but that James's suicide didn't necessarily mean that the case was closed.

More time passed, and the Beaverhead County sheriff failed to produce any "concrete evidence" about the woman's whereabouts. The public was fed the standard line about how the authorities were investigating "any and all leads," which was only one small, mind-numbing step away from telling them that they were "following the course."

"We're trying not to overlook anything," Davis told one newspaper reporter. "Everything is a possibility."

Still, searchers from the police and sheriff's departments and the Beaverhead Search and Rescue Unit failed to locate any trace of the woman. Ground and aerial searches were conducted countywide and regionally, including throughout the open, sparse areas of Argenta, Elkhorn, Stone Creek, and Sweetwater Road.

Fliers about Focher were sent to law enforcement agencies in Montana, as well as several neighboring states. Search dogs from the Montana Canine Academy in Great Falls were added to the search effort.

Davis said that several other local persons were considered "suspects," but until "hard proof" was obtained no arrests would be possible. In the no-nonsense, stern vernacular of the Montana sheriff, he told the media that "he couldn't go and arrest people based solely on a hunch."

FOCHER FOUND WITH SKULL FLATTENED

SOON "HARD PROOF" was furnished in the form of Judith Diane Focher's body, which was found on Saturday, June 21, 1980, in the Big Hole River, near Glen, about thirty miles north of Dillon. According to the coroner, her death was determined to be the result of a skull fracture. The report noted that her head had been struck and flattened by a massive, forceful object, "most likely a full, round vehicle tire," and she suffered manifold abrasions and lacerations to the skull.

ANOTHER PERSON OF INTEREST
NAMED LATER

THE MURDER OF JUDY FOCHER was the kind of crime that people in Dillon would always remember. It disturbed people who saw in her demise an arbitrariness that frightened them, violence unleashed against a defenseless woman without reason. Norm's defenders were staunch and many. Still, he was never able to outrun the rumors and stigmas attached to the circumstances.

In 1987, police started to circulate new fliers and around that time named Matt Pyatt as a person of interest in the murder of Judy Focher. Several years later Pyatt, according to Butte authorities, was heavily questioned in connection with the murder of Julianne Stallman in Butte. Pyatt was linked to both Focher and Stallman through the bars that he once owned, including the Owl Bar in Anaconda and Warm Springs Bar in Warm Springs. Records on file at the Beaverhead County Sheriff's Office describe Pyatt as "feeling a violent antipathy" toward people, especially women, and society. A woman who once dated Pyatt told a private investigator who worked the Focher murder that it was if "a coldness," almost an icy breath, emanated from him. According to his police deposition, Pyatt denied the allegations, and he has never been formally charged with either crime.

Norman Focher passed away on March 17, 2018, at age seventy-six. The laundry business that the Fochers owned no longer exists. There is a 4Bs next door to where the building once stood.

For many years Stan Smith served as the coroner of Beaverhead County, and from time to time he would examine and reexamine the case files of the Focher murder. Similar to others who lived in Dillon at the time of the killing, he has heard his share of rumors and insinuations. What he has seen in the case files, he said, has only heightened his suspicions.

"There are many rumors that went around, and that one alleged suspect (Bill James) killed himself a while later," said Smith. "The other alleged suspect (Matt Pyatt) has never been charged, and the case went cold after that. Her husband left the area eventually. Another rumor was that their marriage was ending."

Smith, who isn't one prone to exaggeration or conspiratorial thinking, said that there is something unnerving about the Focher case—how it was handled, or perhaps even mishandled—that still doesn't sit well in the depths of his stomach. Plenty of dirt on the case has still not been plowed.

"I've often thought that there was somewhat of a coverup or outright neglect that blocked the push to move the investigation further," concluded Smith.

JAMES OTIS ANDERSON

VANISHED: JUNE 13, 1982
VANISHED FROM: TOWNSEND

James Otis Anderson, an Episcopal priest in Broadwater County, gave no indications that he planned to leave for an extended period. His desk and workspace were meticulous—and on the morning of June 13, 1982, he rose at about 6 a.m. and vacuumed the carpets, fixed the lock to the safe, and straightened his bookshelf. The El Corona cigar box that he kept hidden in the closet—in which he stashed a number of wrinkled and very worn $50 bills—ended up on the top of a small pile of books on the floor.

He opened and closed and sifted through a mound of encyclopedias and mass trade Louis L'Amour historical fiction paperbacks and added a couple of dusty Philip K. Dick hardbacks to a stack that, he told his secretary, was bound for the thrift shop. He marked up, in pencil, a rough draft of the day's sermon, the one he was supposed to deliver in a few hours. He erased the last sentence—something about the compassionate comprehension of "lost souls"—and fixed himself a breakfast of tomato soup and dry toast.

He added a few additional comments to the handwritten text of the sermon. And then he made half a pot of coffee. By 7:30 a.m., he was showered and shaved, had his black hair combed, and had his teeth suitably brushed.

He grabbed his suitcase and jumped into his vehicle and at 8 a.m. Anderson was on his way east on Highway 12, leaving Townsend and heading toward White Sulphur Springs. The first service at St. John's Episcopal Church was at 10 a.m. People who saw him didn't think much of it—at first. He had more than enough time to be back at the building, and perhaps he was enjoying the fresh air, enjoying the roads now that they were finally clear of snow and ice.

When the mass commenced James Otis Anderson was nowhere to be seen. He did not speak from the pulpit on that day. In fact, he was never heard from or even seen again.

"TROUBLED" LIFE OF "FATHER JIM"

FULL AND PRECISE ACCOUNTS of the life of James Otis Anderson perhaps may never be told. Born in Wisconsin on March 21, 1928, some people remembered him as a man of warmth and kindness, whereas others described him as "troubled" and a man of loneliness, repression, and sadness. One friend recalled how "Father Jim" planted an apple tree in the backyard of his home as a gift. His humor drew people to him, but it also kept them away. It could be too crude, too inappropriate for certain tastes. Some thought that he got too loud sometimes, too abrasive. One parishioner, more than forty years later, said that she didn't like "his attitude toward girls" and that he was always "thinking about women." Broadwater County Attorney John Flynn once said that "anything was possible with Father Jim."

There was no denying that at the time of his disappearance Anderson was grappling with a very challenging set of personal problems. He had separated from his wife, Patricia Jean O'Connell, and he had filed for divorce, the dissolution of marriage decree listing September 10, 1981, as the separation date. James and Pat married in August 1969, and they had two children, Ian and Shannon; the pair was fighting heavily over custody of them. In addition to his divorce, he was having problems at his job—there were allegations of sexual impropriety with a married adult female—and according to a statement by the Broadwater County sheriff, he "may have been facing termination" from his position in the church. His estranged wife stated he had been acting oddly and that he seemed "distant" and "uncommunicative," which, she said, was one of the problems that led to their separation.

The other thing that prompted the separation was the pastor's strange and secret behavior when it came to the family finances. Six months prior to his disappearance, Anderson had dropped his wife's name from his life insurance and changed the beneficiary to his employer, St. John's Episcopal Church. (The church collected on the policy after he was declared legally dead some years later.)

Authorities surmised that Anderson had hatched a plan either to run away with a secret lover or to end his own life in deep, silent shame. One of the things that bothered investigators was the nature of the personal items of Anderson's that were never located. He had an address book in which he was known to keep copious notes and meticulous details. He almost always had his address book nearby. That address book disappeared. A friend had once given him an Afghan rug— red wine color, made of fine wool—and that rug disappeared. James owned a pistol. He wasn't a hunter, and he wasn't a sportsman. But he had inherited a small-caliber pistol from his father—and that pistol has never been located.

For the next few months, police heavily monitored his credit cards and bank accounts and kept an eye on his Social

Security number. None of these things were ever found to have been used fraudulently.

VOLKSWAGEN FOUND IN ROCKY MOUNTAINS

IN OCTOBER 1982, Anderson's silver 1975 Volkswagen Scirocco was found abandoned in a heavily wooded area of White's Gulch in the Big Belt Mountains, a section of the Rocky Mountains northeast of Townsend. The three-door hatchback appeared to have "been deliberately hidden," according to published records, and investigators said they believed that whoever left it there was familiar with the surrounding area. Obscured by Douglas fir, larch, and spruce trees, it was not visible from the road, the trail, or from the air.

Anderson's ex-wife alleged foul play and she said that he "wasn't a good driver" and she didn't think that he could have driven the car to that remote location on his own. She didn't believe that he walked away on purpose or that he had the desire to take his own life. She said that he had a religious-based opposition to suicide and too much to live for. She maintained that he was a loving, serious father and that he adored his children. Such an ignominious end to his life would have inflicted hurt on them in ways that he wouldn't have allowed. She never ruled out the chance that James was out there somewhere.

But investigators found evidence to support their theory that Anderson had at least been wandering in the area for a while. A search turned up several of Anderson's belongings, including his prayer book, Old Testament Bible, cap, eyeglasses, sinus pills, and clerical collar, all within approximately one mile of the Volkswagen. Some of the items were found on a rocky, exposed ridgeline overlooking Townsend, Canyon

Ferry Lake, and the surrounding area. A bag of additional items, including a gold comb and several empty Dr. Pepper bottles, had been tied to a lodgepole pine either by Anderson or someone who had subsequently discovered them.

LINK TO PEDOPHILE PRIEST MURDER EYED

POLICE COULD FIND no connection between Anderson's case and the unsolved 1984 disappearance of Father John Kerrigan, a Roman Catholic priest who went missing from Ronan and was never found. The two men had worked in White Sulphur Springs at the same time earlier in their clerical careers, and they were reportedly friends. Although Kerrigan's body was never located, enough physical evidence was found in his bloody car to suggest that he had been murdered. Several years ago, the Catholic diocese divulged the sinister truth about Kerrigan following a massive lawsuit by a large number of sexual abuse victims against the diocese. Kerrigan was an inveterate abuser and prolific offender, and he had been shuttled from parish to parish by the diocese, protected and coddled by organizational misfeasance that allowed him to continue his grotesque attacks on children. The exact nature and depth of the friendship between James Otis Anderson and Father John Kerrigan may never be known.

On June 25, 1990, Anderson was declared legally dead, and the Montana certificate of death notes that the Episcopal minister disappeared on or about June 13, 1982.

RANDY CHURCH

MURDERED: FEBRUARY 10, 1985
MURDER LOCATION: BOZEMAN

FEBRUARY 10, 1985. Under the icy, clear winter sky, the Bozeman Pizza Hut at 2300 West Main Street closed and was locked at midnight. Bleak midwinter, and the frosty wind moaned.

Randy Church, a twenty-three-year-old Montana State University student, turned off the front lights and stayed to wash the tables and scrub the ovens. It was a run-of-the-mill Saturday night, a steady spill of customers dining in, mostly college students, and plenty of delivery orders dispersed to dorms across campus and adjacent student housing.

Randy worked about fifteen hours per week at the restaurant, responsibilities he balanced with a full load of electrical and computer engineering courses. Now, he was the shift supervisor, covering the nighttime for a coworker who requested the weekend off.

"A nice fellow with great promise," as his college adviser at Montana State University later described him, Randy was known to contribute when asked, and to be giving with his time. Although two employees should have been paired together at closing time, Randy, "a slow closer," according to one coworker, was in the store by himself.

Sometime around 3 a.m., there was a knock on the rear door of the restaurant. Randy opened the door to face the wintry darkness.

Randy Church, a twenty-three-year-old Montana State University student, was working at Pizza Hut on the night of February 10, 1985. Someone pumped two .22 caliber bullets into his head. Randy was shot first directly below an eye and second, in the back of his head, killing him instantly. His bullet-riddled body was found at approximately 9:30 a.m. the following morning. COURTESY RUBY BURNEY

Suddenly, someone pumped two .22 caliber bullets into his head. Randy was shot the first time directly below an eye, and the second time in the back of his head, killing him instantly. His bullet-riddled body was found at approximately 9:30 a.m. Sunday morning, near the cash register and safe, by business manager Jeff Pierce, after Pierce was called to unlock the doors when Church failed to meet an employee there at 9 a.m.

Sergeant Ron Green of the Bozeman Police Department said the day after the murder that the police were assuming that robbery was the motive for the shooting. He said that police had no suspects and "no idea why Church (wittingly) let the assailant in." Green speculated that Randy, perhaps thinking that friends had stopped by to visit with him after the store had closed, had allowed the perpetrator inside the restaurant. Green said that the store's safe "was not open" and that the total take that morning obtained in taking this young man's life was roughly $1,000.

The autopsy performed on Randy showed no obvious signs of any resistance, Green later said. The restaurant had no alarms, though Green noted that an alarm probably would not have saved Randy in his situation.

Bozeman residents and the family of Randy Church were taken aback over the news of the slaying, "apparently the first murder in Bozeman in more than eight years," according to the *Bozeman Daily Chronicle*. The last murder in Bozeman, according to the *Chronicle*, had occurred in September 1976, when a man named Anthel "Bobo" Brown killed another in a robbery at Hoadley's Standard gas station.

"It was a horrible thing. I can't understand why anyone would do something like that," Randy's uncle, Wesley Church of Havre, told the *Bozeman Daily Chronicle*. "Randy was really a nice young man, always energetic with an exceptional personality. It's a terrible tragedy for the family."

Pizza Hut offered a $1,000 reward for information leading to the arrest and conviction of the person or persons "responsible for this heinous crime." A memorial service was held at the Holland-Bonine Funeral Chapel in Havre and burial followed at the Highland Cemetery. A memorial service was also held at the Danforth Chapel on the MSU campus and a scholarship in Randy's name was funded.

Thirty-five years later, the young man's murder remains a sad, lost footnote in the annals of Bozeman, the sole "uncleared" homicide in the past fifty years on the city's books. Adding to the heartbreak, lead investigator Ron Green believes that he once came face-to-face with Randy's killers and that justice for Randy was squandered in a bureaucratic maze.

THE SENSITIVE, CREATIVE LIFE
OF RANDY CHURCH

RANDY CHURCH was born on September 28, 1961, in Havre to Richard and Darlene Church, the second youngest of their five children. Richard Church, a native of the Harlem area on the Hi-Line, and Darlene, a native of Havre, had married in 1955.

Richard Church supported the family of seven as a machinist with the Great Northern Railway, one of the economic drivers of several small, rural towns like Havre along U.S. Highway 2. Based out of the train repair and refueling station depot in Havre, Richard worked the same shift for many years, 2 to 11 p.m.

Darlene, described as "the loving type" by one of the Church siblings, stayed at home with the children and worked as the main cook at the Pancake House and other local restaurants. Randy clung closely to his mother and often accompanied her to the train depot to deliver Richard his home-cooked dinner.

"Randy was the most sensitive of the siblings," says Rick Church, his older brother. "He was the person who kept the family connected and who could relate to everyone in the family. Dad was a hard guy, and Randy could communicate and connect with everyone, including our father."

Several characteristics defined Randy from the onset of his teens, namely creativity and industriousness. Instead of something store-bought, he would wax his father's car as a birthday present. With eager facility, he shined shoes at a local barbershop. Skinny and modest, Randy was a perfectly ordinary kid who enjoyed goofing off with and chasing his brothers around their property, typically until his asthma forced him to scale it back.

As a teenager, he fell in love with electronics, computers, and the power and torque of muscle cars. His first car was a Dodge Charger, which he used to travel back and forth to his job at the Iron Horse restaurant in Havre. There, Randy was employed as a dishwasher, busboy, and cook; at one point he worked alongside his mother, Darlene, who helped run the kitchen.

"I was one year older than Randy, but we were in the same grade because I got left back," says Randy's brother Robert Church. "We were in the same classes. Randy was always very balanced. I'd come home, and he'd be studying. He could party and still do well in school."

"We used to ride motorbikes together," says Randy's cousin Rusty (who requested that his last name be withheld). "We were pretty close to the same age. What's always stuck out to me the most was when Randy rode his bicycle out here in the summertime, maybe age thirteen or so, forty miles from Havre, twenty miles of pavement, and the rest of gravel. He was one of my best buddies."

Randy attended Northern Montana College for one year (1982–1983) before transferring to Montana State University as an electrical engineering student.

"Randy was extremely intelligent, and he had a heart of gold," says his long-ago friend Gene Meek. "I'm not just saying that because he is deceased. He would help anybody with their studying, their schoolwork. He was kind, and he had an absolute heart of gold."

"One person I thought he always reminded me of a bit was Sonny from Sonny and Cher," says Randy's friend Suzie Williams. "Just from overall physical looks and things; he was really skinny. He loved to ride motorcycles and go out in his blue VW bug and go hill climbing. He owned a '69 green Firebird. We would go motorcycle riding in Havre and the Bear Paw's mountains. I met Randy in a college calculus class in Havre. It was a small class of six kids, and we got to know each other."

Randy's college résumé listed his favorite interests and activities as motorcycling, rafting, and "applying programming knowledge to labor and payroll system needs."

In the fall quarter at Montana State, Randy received three As and one B. He had an overall grade point average of 3.4 and recently had been nominated for the engineering honorary fraternity, Tau Beta Pi. "He worked awfully hard to get through school," said Bruce McLeod, an electrical engineering professor who had Church in two classes in 1985. "He was a typical kid from Montana. He knew how to work and knew what he wanted."

"Randy would've been very excited with these modern computers and smart phones and how they've progressed," recalls his brother Robert Church, who received a letter sent from his brother within days of the crime. "He had a basic computer back then, and he loved technology, and he loved learning about it. He would've loved all of this change. He embraced life."

Randy started working at Pizza Hut in Bozeman in February 1983, advancing from waiter, to cook, to shift supervisor, a position that entailed responsibilities he enjoyed, including controlling the cost of sales and labor and operating expenditures. The job supplied him with money, a concrete work history, and a boost of self-confidence.

Then, one winter night Randy closed the store. Shortly thereafter, someone stole his life, snatched a good deal of money in exchange, and left a smart kid with a positive future murdered in a pool of blood.

ROBBERY AS MOTIVE

POLICE WERE NEVER ABLE TO determine whether Randy was slain because he refused to give the gunman the money, or if the gunman killed Randy so there would not be a witness. According to available police and media reports, the back door of the restaurant had a peephole, but it would have been difficult for Randy to see who was standing outside in the dark.

It appears as if Randy should not have been in the building alone. The assistant manager of the Pizza Hut in Bozeman, Jan Brandon, said in an interview shortly after the crime that "there are supposed to be two people on duty at night, and the back door is supposed to be locked at midnight." Brandon suggested that Randy might have opened the back door thinking it was "probably a fellow employee."

Randy's friend Suzie Williams remembers that one week before Randy was killed, she and her boyfriend, David, an employee at the same Pizza Hut, were startled in the back end of the restaurant by a group of people who appeared after closing time.

"They had come in the side door after closing," says Suzie. "Someone had gone out the side door earlier that day and it didn't latch correctly. Unless it was something extremely personal no one knew about, I couldn't think of any reason someone would want to do that to Randy."

It's possible that since Randy was supposed to be opening the next morning, he intended to stay at the restaurant overnight and that he was working on homework when the intruder entered.

Bill Davis of Billings, at the time the regional director of Pizza Hut, told the Associated Press in 1985 that Pizza Huts "in large inner cities" had alarm buttons that employees could push to notify police. But that system was yet to be in effect in Pizza Huts in Montana or Wyoming because crime rates in those states were not "high enough to warrant it."

The restaurant's bank bag and approximately twenty-five checks in a vinyl bag were found later in a ditch on Jackrabbit Lane near Belgrade. There also was a theft of $911 at the Town Pump in Bozeman reported the Sunday morning that Randy was killed.

LOCAL SUSPECTS IDENTIFIED

MICHAEL NICKELSON, nineteen, of Livingston was named as a suspect in the Randy Church killing after he was taken into custody for the slaying of a coworker at Yellowstone National Park. In the summer of 1985, Nickelson beat to death Randy Dean Reddog of Wolf Point near Old Faithful in Yellowstone. Bozeman Police Sergeant Stan Kenney said that an inmate "who met Nickelson while they both were in custody" alerted authorities that Nickelson had told him that he was involved in the Pizza Hut murder.

Kenney said that police "were not able to prove that Nickelson was at the crime scene," and that Nickelson "refused to discuss it." Nickelson was charged with—and later convicted of—an armed robbery of the Heritage Inn in Bozeman several weeks after the Pizza Hut homicide. Later convicted of the park slaying, Nickelson was never charged in connection with Randy's death.

Soon after Randy's homicide, police questioned James Livermore, twenty-five, a man arrested in Livingston and charged with robbing a gas station there on February 9, 1985. In that incident, Livermore menaced the clerk of a Town Pump with a pistol and fled with $700. Authorities, however, could find

no apparent connection between the robbery of the Livingston Town Pump and the shooting of Randy Church in Bozeman the next day. Two .22-caliber shells found at Pizza Hut
could not be conclusively matched with the ballistics of the
pistol that Livermore used.

NEW MEXICO PRISON ESCAPEES

RAY B. SCHRIVNER, fifty-three, and Mark St. Clair, thirty-seven, escaped from a state prison in Albuquerque, New
Mexico, on January 7, 1985. St. Clair was serving thirty years
for the murder of a New Mexico deputy sheriff, and Schrivner
was serving twenty years for armed robbery and kidnapping.
The two men stole a beige 1983 Mazda in Colorado and
headed north from New Mexico through Montana to Saskatchewan, Canada, and were believed to have entered Canada north of Plentywood or Wolf Point.

The duo crossed the border the day after Randy was killed
and were eventually arrested on February 21, 1985, by the
Royal Canadian Mounted Police (RCMP) near Nipawin, Saskatchewan, near the city of Prince Albert.

A map authorities found in their vehicle had a route drawn
on it from Colorado, where the vehicle was stolen, through
Montana, entering Montana on Highway 87 southeast of
Billings and continuing west to Bozeman. Several witnesses
later claimed to have seen two similar looking strangers in
the vicinity.

Sergeant Ron Green thought that the snowy tire tracks
left at the Pizza Hut would be worth matching against the
escapees' vehicle; if the outlined map he had been informed
of could definitely place them near Bozeman the night of

February 10, 1985, he would have a hot lead. The escapee's fingerprints were sent to the state crime lab in Missoula to check against prints taken at the scene. The results of these tests are unknown.

Green traveled to Prince Albert on March 18, 1995, to interview Schrivner and St. Clair. According to Green, he flew from Bozeman to Winnipeg, and then to Saskatoon, Saskatchewan, where he was escorted to Nipawin by the RCMP.

According to Detective Green, the duo seemed like the most likely suspects, linked by the map, as well as the shoeprints and tire tracks similar to those gathered at the crime scene, and finally, their own incriminating statements.

"It was at a time of a recent snowfall so car tracks, footprints were easily photographed," says Ron Green, in 2020. "In the car was a map from Colorado to Montana. [The map went] from Billings to Bozeman, Montana, back to Billings, and crossing at the Canadian Border, near Plentywood, Montana. Not sure how they managed to cross the border . . . The RCMP called asking about crimes that had happened in Montana. After an interview with the suspects and getting certain information that they should not have known, seeing the shoes they were wearing and the tires on the car, I was certain they were involved. [We] brought the tires back on the plane and other info. This was all turned over to County Attorney Marty Lambert, and items were sent to the FBI."

The two fugitives fought against their extradition and lost. Green says that upon return to the United States, the suspects were first held in North Dakota and then released to the custody of New Mexico authorities.

"The Gallatin County attorney, Marty Lambert, decided not to bring them to Bozeman for a hearing," says Green.

"They were being returned to prison in New Mexico, and they were being charged for escape and had to finish out the original life in prison charges."

According to information obtained from the public information officer at the New Mexico Corrections Department, both Schrivner and St. Clair died "of natural causes" in prison.

NOT A "COLD UNSOLVED CASE"

OFFICER GREEN planned to retire from the Bozeman Police Department in May 1985 but stayed on the job longer, hoping to close the books on the Randy Church murder.

"I really did believe they [the New Mexico prison escapees] were involved," said Green in 2020. "Without my testimony at a hearing, I was lost and felt it was the [Gallatin] County attorney [Marty Lambert] who did not want to waste his time if they were returning to prison."

"I do not view this as a cold, unsolved case," Green continued. "A hearing would have resolved this one way or the other. After my retirement, many detectives had tried to reopen the case without any new information to solving this. I am saddened by the fact this is still a cold case and, yes, I am reminded many times about this case without ever being able to testify."

Despite his strong inclination, Green concedes that there was not as much substantive evidence as he would have liked to pin the New Mexico men to the crime—no witnesses, no ballistics, no confessions, and no weapon. Perhaps further obscuring the mystery of Randy's death, police have never officially eliminated other suspects, including a man "who served time in Wisconsin for murder," according to available police and media reports, and who "was in Bozeman at the time of the shooting and who knew Church."

According to emails obtained between Bozeman authorities and members of the Church family, a remaining person of interest in the case is one of Randy's co-employees at Bozeman Pizza Hut, someone who moved into the apartment at 301 W. Story in Bozeman that Randy vacated shortly before his murder. On top of this, Bozeman authorities contacted several of Randy's siblings in 2015 about obtaining a DNA sample, "to help separate the DNA from the crime scene, but then they never followed up," says Rick Church.

Time and time again leads were established, yet no charges in the killing of Randy Church were ever levied against anyone, a pattern deemed cruel and insufficient by his family and friends. Questioned about the media and police reports corroborating Green's time line of activities, Marty Lambert, now in his sixth term as Gallatin County attorney, declined to comment on the murder of Randy Church. He did say that he was "a homicide victim" and that he needed "to get conversant again in the status of the case and the investigation."

"It's almost a daily occurrence that Randy is a part of some thought," says his friend Suzie Williams. "I wonder what it would be like for him to still be around, and what he would've done."

Randy's sister, Ruby Burney, says that her multiple questions about the lack of transparency in Randy's death have yet to be answered.

"Why would you do that to him and his family? His mother and father didn't get the answers they needed. Why is it that everybody has apparently forgotten about this case? I can't forget about this case. It's a part of my life."

A FATHER'S HAUNTING WORDS

Two years after Randy's murder, his father, Richard Church, told the Associated Press he had "little hope" that authorities would ever track down and punish those who murdered his son. His bitterness was palpable.

"If they do find the guy, they won't do anything about it," Richard Church was quoted as saying. "They'll throw him in prison and feed the sucker. And that ain't good enough in my book. . . . They should catch the guy and give him the same medicine he gave my son . . . and I'd like to do it."

Richard, who died in 2010, made sure he had his tombstone connected with Randy's at the cemetery. Randy's mother, Darlene, died in 2017. Three of Randy's four siblings each named one of their children after their lost brother.

"If there is one thing in this world I would change, it would be going back to that Saturday night," says his brother Robert Church. "I'd somehow go back to that Saturday night and get him out of there before he got killed."

BEN BURNS

MURDERED: MARCH 11, 1986
MURDER LOCATION: BILLINGS

ON MARCH 11, 1986, the body of an unknown white man was discovered on Pryor Creek Road outside Billings at around 12:30 a.m. The man had been shot twice in the head. One bullet pierced his forehead, and another blew apart a portion of his jaw.

The body, "languished in the morgue," according to an official police statement, until the victim was identified as Benjamin Burns, age twenty.

Police said that he was identified through "his clothing"— gold bell bottoms, a brown snap-button floral shirt with chrysanthemums—and a distinctive tattoo of his initials on his upper right arm and a self-inflicted marking of a skull over a cross on his upper left arm.

Details about the life of the victim were exasperatingly vague: Ben Burns was "a resident of Forsyth, Montana," who had "unspecified business" in Missoula.

VAGUE, HAZY COMPOSITE OF VICTIM

TWO WEEKS AFTER his body was discovered, his identification card was found in a pile of shattered glass on I-94 between Billings and Huntley. A piece of jewelry was found near the identification card—a sterling silver ring initialed and stamped by a blacksmith in north central Montana—but it was never positively identified as belonging to Burns. However, investigators are "fairly confident," in their words, that several other items of evidence in storage connect to the victim. But they've refused from the beginning to name them.

Police on both sides of the state teamed up to build a composite of Burns—and that sketch was a vague and hazy one. He seemed to have run away from his family as a teenager and only contacted them occasionally in recent years. But he did return every now and again to visit with an on-again, off-again girlfriend and one of his female cousins. He wasn't enrolled at the University of Montana. He worked two jobs to make ends meet in Missoula. He picked up short-term farm and agricultural tasks through one of the job corps. The jobs ranged from loading lumber to slogging and stacking cowhides at a plant on Mullan Road, which then shipped them to various cosmetics plants in Spokane. At one point, he worked at the city newspaper as an agate clerk for the sports desk.

On March 11, 1986, police determined that he spent the day hitchhiking, destined to visit the occasional girlfriend and female cousin in Forsyth. He was believed to have hitchhiked between Forsyth and Missoula several times. With the perfect clarity of hindsight, hitchhiking would today be considered one of the most impulsive and unwise things that one could do, but at the time it wasn't widely frowned upon, and not too many young people were worried about it contributing to a horrible outcome. Burns had always been a lucky hitchhiker. He would always get a ride immediately. When he reached the Higgins Street Bridge in Missoula the first car along stopped to pick him up. The driver was a retired grocer on his way to the Bearmouth Chalet.

"He was a young man who hitchhiked at a time when people his age were casually hitchhiking," said Sergeant Dan Paris of the Yellowstone County Sheriff's Office in 2023. "He was not at odds with anyone as far as we know. No grudges against him. He wasn't someone who had somebody tracking him or following him or waiting for an opportunity to harm him. He just got into the wrong vehicle."

Paris said that investigators were able to determine the man's itinerary of travel on the day of his murder, the more than 442 miles of interstate that Burns journeyed. Several drivers later came forward with information and said that they'd provided him with a ride along certain legs. But the final driver—the one who transported him to Billings—has never been located, and Paris said investigators would be most interested in locating and speaking with that person.

Bancroft said that not much else of note about the Burns case would be helpful to the public. He said that the area where Burns was found was not far from the Parker Golf Course; and the bar, clubhouse, and maintenance buildings were only about five hundred feet away. But no one there reported hearing or seeing anything suspicious. Residents had heard gunshots shortly before the body was discovered. But no one in the area saw or reported anything of value—a speeding car or distinct license plate, an unusual vehicle with menacing hallmarks, a motorist changing a flat, or even someone loitering near an underpass a minute or two too long.

Robbery is the suspected motive for the crime. If this is true, according to an official police statement, Ben would have died for "less than a dollar in change." Another possible motive was sexual assault: Burns might have fallen prey to an unwanted advance from a cruising, predatory male and things went horribly twisted from there. Paris that it could be one or the other or neither of the two, which is what makes the case most challenging.

Anyone with information regarding the murder of Ben Burns may contact the Yellowstone County Sheriff's Office Cold Case Unit at (406) 869-3530.

TIMOTHY KIMBRELL

VANISHED: NOVEMBER 29, 1987
VANISHED FROM: SAN FRANCISCO

TIMOTHY KIMBRELL was born in Columbia Falls and grew up in nearby Kalispell, the youngest of three siblings. In school, teachers lauded the plucky kid with good grades, sometimes calling him by his middle name, Oscar. They also noticed a precocious tendency to shout down bullies and shoo them away from prey. He was tall and muscular and sometimes found himself standing up for his older sisters. His upbringing seemed like a happy one: an Eagle Scout who raced on his parents' sailboats, cycled competitively in high school, played several instruments, and built elaborate model airplanes. He attended the University of Montana and later transferred to California State University in Fullerton.

THROES OF MENTAL BREAKDOWN

AT AGE THIRTY-FOUR, Timothy Kimbrell, however, was in the throes of a series of serious mental health issues. The Kalispell native was living in San Francisco in November 1987 when he broke up with his girlfriend and became severely depressed. She moved out of the little two-room apartment they had shared on Jones Street, overlooking Alcatraz.

A few months earlier, he had lost a sibling to leukemia. On November 8, 1987, he was involved in a car accident and ticketed for not stopping at a red light. Then he and his girlfriend broke up. Shortly thereafter, he told his boss at the telephone company that he had been stricken by a disease and had no reason to live. He said he was going to quit, sell his belongings, and give the money to needy people for Thanksgiving. His boss talked him out of it, and Timothy continued to work at the accounts receivable department, crunching numbers.

On Sunday, November 29, 1987, he spent the morning at a thrift store and a community medical center where he told the nurse that he had debilitating anxiety and "had had enough," according to documents provided by the Kalispell Police Department. He called his boss at home. He asked him to mail his last paycheck to his mother, Vanetta, in Kalispell. He calmly provided the address. His boss tried to dissuade him from quitting. But Timothy said that he had his mind fixed. He went upstairs and told his neighbor that he was heading to Hollywood Hills in the morning. He had a few travel books that belonged to the San Francisco Public Library, and he took them right to the library and dropped them in the night-deposit box.

Sometime in the evening, he met friends in a bar in the Haight-Ashbury district, according to reports from the investigation. He talked about pop cinema and records and about his mother and the weather. She lived in Montana, where it was snowing furiously. He hated the weather in Montana. But the sunshine in San Francisco was sporadic, not nearly as prevalent as he had wished. When it was supposed to be summer in the Bay City, it was cold and foggy.

It was, however, an oddly sunny evening in November. No rain. No wind. At the bar, he had four cans of beer. He looked nervous, his friends reported. He had tics when he was nervous—grunting, handwringing, wincing, and uncontrolled blinking. He said he was worried that his mother would never receive the check. His friends split into groups: some stayed at the bar, and the remainder of the group was going to search for discounted disco records. Timothy said he wanted to be alone. A telephone booth was on the corner. He said he was going to step out and call his mother. Looking wan and bleary-eyed, he staggered out onto the street.

Timothy's mother received the check, but she never heard from Timothy again. No one ever heard from Timothy again.

CAR FOUND; WHEREABOUTS FOREVER UNKNOWN

ON AUGUST 6, 1989, San Francisco police impounded an abandoned vehicle registered in Kimbrell's name, but authorities found no sign of foul play or evidence that shed any light on the mystery. His mother reported to authorities in August 1991 that she had received a call from a man claiming to be her son but that she didn't recognize the voice and dismissed the call as harassment. "We've tried to run him down every which way you can think of and have been unable to determine his whereabouts," Kalispell Police Detective Gene Holliday told a San Francisco newspaper.

The Kalispell Police Department said that the folder on Timothy hasn't been reviewed in decades: manila, sandy with dust, unused, and jaundice yellow from the vagaries of time and age.

"There isn't a whole lot that we could have done back then to look for him," said a spokesperson for the Kalispell Police Department. "It's crazy how someone could just disappear that way. With no one looking for him, it's kind of like he never existed. It was easier to disappear back then if you wished to."

HALLIE GANJE

MURDERED: MAY 18, 1991
MURDER LOCATION: LIVINGSTON

SATURDAY, MAY 18, 1991. At approximately 12:15 a.m., sixteen-year-old Hallie Ganje sat on the bank of the Yellowstone River in Livingston near the Ninth Street Bridge. She unzipped her black and white striped handbag and yanked out a cigarette, lit it, and took a drag in the blackness.

Hallie's purse contained her McDonald's work uniform, an assortment of cosmetics, a few photographs of herself and her friends, and, given that she was noted as the DJ among her friends, about a dozen cassette tapes. Tucked in one pouch was a Greyhound bus ticket in her name for an upcoming trip to Oregon, where she planned to visit a friend.

She smoked one cigarette down to the base, then another. A cluster of flicked Marlboro Reds—her favorite—encircled the bench where she perched.

She sat in the darkness for many minutes, perhaps self-interrogating her life in sober and calculated tones. Inexplicably, she had just abruptly walked away from a party a few blocks away. Following an argument, her sunny mood went into eclipse. Hallie was known to sink occasionally into a crestfallen disposition, so perhaps a walk in the night air would improve her frame of mind, soften her mood.

Only Hallie could've known what Hallie felt, saw, or heard that night. She would certainly have paid attention to the

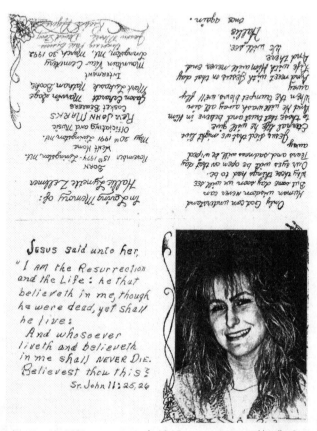

On Saturday, May 18, 1991, at approximately 12:15 a.m., sixteen-year-old Hallie Ganje sat at the banks of the Yellowstone River in Livingston near the Ninth Street Bridge. Ten months later, a Livingston area rancher spotted a skeleton among debris deposited on an island in the Yellowstone River. Through dental records, forensics identified the young woman's remains. The condition of the skeleton, according to the Yellowstone County Coroner, appeared consistent with someone who had been in the river for about a year. AUTHOR'S COLLECTION/PUBLIC DOMAIN

furious interplay of the Yellowstone waters, perhaps with something akin to fright, for she harbored a terrible fear of water.

Ten months later, a Livingston area rancher spotted a skeleton among debris deposited on an island in the Yellowstone River. Through dental records, forensics identified the young woman's remains as sixteen-year-old Hallie Lynette Ganje. The condition of the skeleton, according to the Yellowstone County coroner, appeared consistent with the remains of someone who had been in the river for about a year.

THE FINAL NIGHTS OF HALLIE GANJE

THE STORY OF THE END of Hallie Ganje's life overlaps with a party at the family home of Chris Gilberg on Ninth Street Island. While Chris's parents were on vacation, Chris decided to throw a massive, multiday event. All he needed was an abundance of booze and a quantity of bodies to show up and consume it. He succeeded on both counts.

"Chris was a loner, a very strange guy," says David Story, who arranged the party from which Hallie Ganje left minutes before she died. "I didn't know him before the party. He came into my workplace, and he asked me to throw it, because he knew that I was popular."

According to Story, who was twenty-one at the time, the party kicked off sometime Friday evening and after a raging, alcohol-saturated Saturday night, cooled down by Sunday afternoon.

"We invited a ton of people over to their house," says Story, a native of California who now lives in Colorado. "There had to have been fifty or sixty people there over a two or three-day weekend. On Saturday afternoon, my friends were going out on a beer run, because we were running out of alcohol. When they returned, there were two girls with them, and one of them was Hallie Ganje. They had a bunch of alcohol to unload from the vehicle. Hallie donated $100 to the beer run."

It was the underage Ganje, "a lightweight" drinker compared to her friends, who helped stoke the party at the house.

Hallie cut a striking and rebellious figure, her blonde hair swept upward, wrapped in the hairspray-drenched style characteristic of the eighties. She had green eyes and wore heavy black eyeliner, reinforcing one of her friend's descriptions of Hallie as "the type of teenager who wouldn't leave the house without makeup."

She was "absolutely beautiful," according to some, yet she didn't believe it. Her compulsion about her looks was a form of undoing.

"Hallie was friendly, shy, a really pretty girl," says Story of the teenager. "We had a relationship for two days, or however long the party was. I considered her my 'girlfriend.'"

David Story concedes that from the start of the investigation into Hallie's death, he was considered one of the top suspects. Almost thirty years later, he admits that his recollection of Hallie's final night is murky and at places inconsistent. But he adamantly maintains that he has no knowledge as to how, when, or why she died.

A FRACTURED EVENING

JESSICA BREWER was the friend who attended the party with Hallie. Following Brewer's recollections, along with Story's memories from the weekend, a time line of events emerges. Considering the mind-altering substances used over the weekend, it is not surprising that accounts vary about exactly what may have happened.

According to Brewer and Story, the party may well have coincided with Hallie's first day of work at the local McDonald's. She might have even come to the party wearing a

McDonald's uniform or she might have changed out of it in the car on the way to the house. She was drinking heavily on Saturday night; and though she wasn't taking heavy drugs or hallucinogenics, she was probably smoking marijuana.

Sometime on Saturday night, Jessica Brewer says there was an argument (Story doesn't recall it, but he doesn't deny that it could have happened) between Hallie and a local teenager, someone whom she "might have (previously) fooled around with," by the name of James Hayes.

According to Brewer and police statements made by witnesses, James Hayes and his brother Joshua showed up uninvited to the Ninth Street Island party. There was strife, shouting, and at one point, a prolonged confrontation between the two or perhaps even three of the Hayes brothers and Hallie and David Story.

At one point, James and Joshua Hayes, "rough and loud party boys with not a good reputation," according to one witness, "rifled through Hallie's personal belongings," and "she demanded that the brothers leave." The altercation ended with the brothers storming out in a huff and Hallie weeping, according to Brewer. The altercation upset Hallie.

"She was crying and talking about what an asshole James Hayes was," says Brewer. "She decided to walk to her sister's house on Ninth Street. I stayed there at the [party] house, and that was the last time I'd seen her."

The evening has haunted Brewer ever since.

"It's scary. There is a dark scariness here in Livingston," Brewer says.

After the fight ended, Hallie either stayed a few more hours with David Story (according to his account), or a distraught Hallie left at some point afterward (according to Jessica Brewer). Per available police reports, Brewer said that she "walked with Hallie to the Ninth Street Bridge," though Brewer denies ever making such a statement.

Story says that later that night, he offered Hallie a ride home—probably about 9 p.m., he estimates—but she would not accept it. He needed to be at work the following morning at 9 a.m. at Western Drug and wanted to get as much sleep as possible.

"I told her, I'm not getting up at 6:30 in the morning to drive you home before I have to go to work," says Story. "She was so adamantly against it [leaving the party]. She lived about forty-five minutes away, somewhere near Pray, I think."

At about midnight, Hallie jiggled Story from sleep. She might have had a few beers between 9 p.m. and midnight, says Story, or she could have been sitting there in the corner watching him sleep for a few hours.

According to Story, Hallie agitatedly told him that she had an aunt who lived "right across the bridge on Ninth Street." He says he strongly resisted being awakened. But Hallie needed to leave without delay, and she would stay nowhere else but at her aunt's house. Story said that he bade her farewell. Hallie scribbled down her phone number on a scrap of paper, Story says, and vanished from the room.

On Sunday morning, Story says he left the house to start work at Western Drug. He walked through the house, past Chris Gilberg, the party host, who was sleeping on a couch, and surveyed the cumulative damage from the weekend of revelry.

"I thought, my god, these people are going to sue me for their house! It was trashed. It was an expensive, fancy house. I was worried about that house that everyone had utterly destroyed. They must have had to work two days to have to clean that. I never returned to the house, or saw the kid, Chris, again."

As it turned out, Hallie had lied to her parents and said she was planning to spend Saturday and Sunday night at the home of her friend, Amber Stringfellow. When she didn't return home Monday, Hallie was reported missing by her mother, Cheryl Standish.

Hallie never showed up for work at McDonald's, and a check her mother had given her for $10 either for lunch or to pay for her uniform shirt, Hallie had altered to $100 to spend on alcohol.

HALLIE'S SHADOW SIDE

A VERY DIFFERENT, far darker world emerges when viewing Hallie from the descriptions of those who knew her at sixteen: a young woman full of self-contempt, distrust, secrets, doom, and terrible sadness.

Initially, authorities suspected that Hallie might have run away to Casper, Wyoming, with a friend named Ricky Pollock, a struggling drug addict employed as a cook at a popular café and biker bar.

"Police immediately said that she was only a sixteen-year-old troubled runaway, and they just wrote her off," says her friend Sunshine Zumwalt. "They gave up on her immediately— within a day it seemed. They said that she had problems and that she ran away with Ricky Pollock. It's a terrible shame on them."

Pollock says that he remembers "FBI guys surrounding me at work before she was found."

"She wore good-looking short miniskirts, and I think she liked the attention," says Ricky Pollock, now fifty-one and living in Bozeman. "I wouldn't say that she was an airhead. She was very naive, and the naivete and the short miniskirts probably didn't help, but I don't know. At the time of her death, I was doing drugs, mostly meth, and I had to get away from Livingston to get off it, to recover. After she was missing, I heard that she was going to my house. Livingston cops and her mom said that. We kind of went out, and she kind of was my girlfriend, I guess."

A pattern in Hallie's young life is that she frequently partied and drank with older guys, like Pollock, like Story, people even ten years or more her senior. Male attention appeared to have been the dominant theme of her self-therapy.

Born November 15, 1974, the daughter of Kenneth Zellmer and Cheryl Standish, Hallie had some minor encounters with the local authorities, including a summons for being a minor in possession of alcohol. She grew up in the Pine Creek area in Paradise Valley south of Livingston and attended junior high and high school in Livingston. For lack of options, she spent a lot of time after school at the bowling alley—the quintessential small-town hangout. Her weekends were spent playing video games and pool and shrugging off the hours with her friends.

Some of Hallie's friends partied thunderously. She tried marijuana but mostly stuck to casual underage drinking. She hung around older boys—men, really—the type who even in their twenties and even thirties saw nothing wrong in their relationships with teenage girls such as Hallie.

Indeed, Hallie's lack of self-confidence often drove her to make questionable choices, such as exchanging fawning letters with a convicted murderer named Richie Allen Ayers. Hallie told her friends that she didn't believe that Ayers, convicted in 1991 of raping and murdering a Livingston woman, was guilty, and that he should not have been sent to prison.

"Hallie was an extremely insecure person," says Sunshine Zumwalt. "She was very eager to please, very young, very easily led. . . . She was insecure, and she would bring her hand up in front of her face to talk, hiding behind it. She was meek. Not a spunky girl. Very, very shy. I can't think of anything that would make anyone want to hurt her."

Hallie's family was left with a dearth of clues as to what had happened to her: the handbag found next to the Ninth Street Island Bridge, a bench with (according to police reports) "two sets of footprints," and "a circle of cigarette butts."

Although her relationship with men was often somewhat predatory with her as prey, Hallie was fortunate to have a number of authentic friendships with female peers. One of them was Anita Hughes. Hallie moved in with Anita and her family when the two were junior high school students.

"She was funny, and that was part of who she was," says Anita. "She would be airheaded a lot and make us laugh because she would say off-the-wall things. But what surprised me about her was that she had trophies for winning spelling bees and that kind of stuff. Whenever we were outside, she always kept her hand in front of her face when she smiled and laughed. She kept her hands in her sleeves and her hand up in front of her face. She thought that her nose was big and that she had an ugly smile. She did not! She had pretty green eyes."

Still, Hughes says, "She wouldn't leave the house without makeup. She didn't like her picture taken."

"My picture and the bus ticket were there in the handbag (left behind at the bridge)," adds Anita, who left Montana for Oregon in 1990. "At first her mom thought that she had run away. . . . The things I heard about her afterwards were bullshit. I know that she was shy with her body, that she didn't think that she was pretty. Before she died, she couldn't wait to come to Oregon and [for us] to see one another."

THE AFTERMATH

ACCORDING TO DAVID STORY, he worked at Western Drug from 9 a.m. to 6 p.m. on Monday, May 20, 1991, and at 6:15 p.m. he walked into the Livingston Police department and wrote and signed a statement. He was asked to come to the station to help find the missing girl. There he filed a deposition and was on his way home in a matter of minutes.

"That's when her mom said that Hallie didn't have an aunt living off of Ninth Street," says Story. "She stole and forged a check, and she never showed up to her first day of work, and she lied about visiting her aunt. This was never a murder case. Mom was matter of fact that she killed herself. The cigarette butts identified as hers were found near the bench, and there was no doubt that she was at that bench.

"I wrote out a small paragraph and a half of a statement. Being the last person who was with her in a boyfriend-girl-friend way, you would think that they would want more information. But, no, for some reason, those ten minutes that I was in the police station many, many years ago were enough."

It is true that Hallie was having difficulties in her home life, even seeking legal emancipation from her parents. Her friends said that she frequently "couch surfed for weeks on end." Hallie's intended destination that night, if she had one, was most likely the home of Amber Stringfellow, who lived nearby on Eighth Street. Amber had been grounded by her parents and she couldn't attend the party at the Island, though her mother agreed to allow Hallie to stay with them that night. On Saturday morning, Amber and Hallie talked on the telephone for several minutes.

They would never speak again.

Ten months later, Hallie Ganje was found in the Yellowstone River and pronounced dead by Park County coroner Albert C. Jenkins at 12:32 p.m. on March 3, 1992. Jenkins listed the immediate cause of death as "unknown."

From the time she vanished, many of Hallie's friends and family reacted with suspicion. Why would the intensely private Hallie dump out a bag with all her personal belongings next to the river on the ground? Weren't the scattered cigarette butts a hint that she was obviously waiting for someone?

"I think that the police thought that she just ran away, and they didn't look at the river," says Hallie's half-sister Angel Colman. "They treated her as a runaway. Nine months later, they found her. There were people who would say that they saw her in different places, like at the mall. There's not a lot of faith in the police here. They didn't even listen to my mom, who immediately thought that she was in the river. They just blew her off about that."

Some of Hallie's friends and family were still convinced that Hallie was murdered. Nearly thirty years later, the question still elicits the same reaction.

"I taught her how to doggie paddle when she was about fifteen," says her friend Amber Stringfellow. "She was absolutely terrified of water. Never would she have gone in the water!"

"She didn't like water because she didn't like to get her hair wet or her makeup to come off," says friend Anita Hughes. "She wouldn't let anything go above her shoulders. She and I played in the water before. But she was afraid of the river because it could get wild certain times of the year. Somebody killed her. It never added up. It wasn't her to kill herself."

Hallie's plans to visit Hughes in Oregon always remained as evidence in her friend's mind that Hallie's thinking at the time of her death was level-headed and clear and even optimistic.

"She was planning on coming out to see my daughter, who was one month old. We talked every week and would write each other every day. . . . What people said doesn't match up to her."

No arrests were ever made in connection with the death of Hallie Ganje. Yet according to an email exchange between former Livingston Police Captain Eric Severson and one of Hallie's friends, over the years the Livingston police reinterviewed James Hayes, who was involved in the argument with Hallie before her death.

As stated in the email exchange, "There is no doubt that James Hayes killed Hallie Ganje," wrote Captain Severson. "He did it. He was the one to have gone after."

James Hayes jumped to his death from a bridge over a river on May 28, 2005, in Missouri. One of his siblings, Joshua Hayes, who allegedly caused the disturbance at the party, has an arrest record that includes charges of theft, domestic battery, and aggravated assault for menacing a woman with a loaded handgun. According to available public records, at one point in the mid-1990s, James, Joshua, and their younger brother, Brian Hayes, were all on probation simultaneously in Park County. Their father, a convicted violent and drug offender, James Richard Hayes, died February 4, 2018.

David Story says that his initial impression of what might have happened to Hallie was informed by the Livingston police and some members of Hallie's family.

"At the time, the police painted this picture," says Story. "So, here's a girl, she didn't show up to work, was having problems with her family, had emotional problems, was worried, sitting by the bridge, with no one to give her a ride home. She stole money from her mom. She had all of this baggage I didn't know about. She barely spoke three words to me from the time I met her."

Story saved a copy of his initial police statement. In it he avows that he wasn't the final person to see Hallie before she left the house party, that it was Chris Gilberg, the party host.

"If something happened, if Hallie left, she must have walked past Chris, who was sleeping on the couch, who had called it as his place to sleep. Chris must be involved in some way with the suspicion of Hallie Ganje going missing. Originally, he said that she walked by, and she said good-bye to him, and she left. He called me at Western Drug, he said that he saw Hallie, and he spoke to her; and then said he never saw her leave . . . wrote a police report, and I never heard a thing about it until about ten years ago.

"A cop from Livingston called who said that he was looking through several old cases, said that he was trying to get a new perspective on them. He never said cold case. Up until then, I'd always assumed that she killed herself."

Story says that he often attempts to envision the darkness that engulfed Hallie on that final night, not just the physical shadows of the night but the mental gloom that may have influenced her mood.

"She had stood there for a while, and she was probably wondering what she was going to do. . . . There was evidence that she was sitting there wondering what to do for three or four cigarette butts worth of time. Her parents had problems with Hallie for years, even committed her to a place. . . . She must have been under immense shame and guilt. She was beside herself with depression and sadness, and she jumped into the Yellowstone River, and that was the end of it."

Despite everything that supports the theory of Hallie committing suicide, Story says that several conspicuous elements of the case have always sowed enough doubt in his mind that she was guilty of her own death. Yes, her insecurities rattled and raked her, but when he thinks back, his logic isn't fixated on suicide.

"If I had given her a ride home, maybe she would be here, and everything would be all right. Or maybe, if I'd have given her a ride home, we'd both be dead."

JENNIFER PENTILLA

VANISHED: OCTOBER 17, 1991
VANISHED FROM: DEMING, NEW MEXICO

"Hi, Mom, I have a change of plans." These were the first words out of the mouth of eighteen-year-old Missoula teenager Jennifer Pentilla on October 17, 1991—and her mother was relieved to hear them.

She had boarded a flight with her bicycle a few weeks earlier destined for California, determined to ride to Mexico to join fellow aid workers as part of a humanitarian project for children. At 7:52 a.m., on October 17, 1991, she leaned against the pay phone outside the Downtown Shell station on Pine Street in Deming, New Mexico, an isolated agricultural town of cattle, chili peppers, onions, and melons.

Thin, blonde, and alone, she was last seen wearing a lightweight pair of blue and white biking gloves and brown hiking boots, a slim chain with a cross emblem dangled around her neck, her blue eyes obscured by dark brown eyeglasses. Plunked in the barrenness of the desert, she stood thirty-five miles north of the Mexican border, approximately 1,350 miles south of her Montana home.

She believed in the alms of humanitarian work, which allowed her to celebrate her faith that at times in her life she had been compelled to camouflage. In fact, she had visited Mexico a few months earlier, where she had spent a part of her summer painting and repairing old churches; and a few

At 7:52 a.m., on October 17, 1991, eighteen-year-old Missoula teenager Jennifer Pentilla leaned against the pay phone outside the Downtown Shell station on Pine Street in Deming, New Mexico, an isolated agricultural town of cattle, chili peppers, onions, and melons. She was never seen again. On September 4, 1992, a pair of dove hunters found her backpacks, a bicycle helmet, a blue and gray tent, and a set of her handwritten journals. Her bicycle was never found. COURTESY LINDA BLUMER

years before that, at the end of her junior year at Great Falls High School, she had traveled without a chaperone to work in Sierra Leone, West Africa—cleaning brush, chopping timber, tilling land—sometimes doing more than one job at a time.

Now she felt that it would be safer to modify her plans, not to venture south. Once Jennifer made the decision, she was disinclined to revisit it. And though her mother, Lynn, respected her daughter's independence and the implacable sense of faith that balanced it, "Mom, I have a change of plans" was a decision that she wanted to hear.

To Lynn, Jennifer seemed like a good girl trying to figure it all out and having a little trouble along the way, especially after the recent loss of her father, Nick Pentilla, who had died of leukemia at age forty-four. She seemed thoughtful, confident, and above all, hopeful. Moreover, she had always had the strength of character to be accountable for her behavior.

Lynn had lost much sleep and had had several bad dreams since her daughter had flown to San Diego on October 1. Further, she had even experienced pangs of guilt because Jennifer was traveling riskily while employing a mountain bike and camping equipment that Lynn had bought for her as high school graduation gifts only months before.

Jennifer worked hard to make the most of such freedom. Two weeks camping and bike riding in the unfamiliar West and Southwest, with stops in Campo, California, and Willcox, Arizona, as well as in Mexico, including, most recently, Tecate, where at times she relied on strangers for car rides and even shelter. "Faith is not faith until it's all you're holding onto," was a credo that she had just scratched in her journal.

Still, Lynn intuited the turbulence in Jennifer's voice. Perhaps her daughter—a gentle child, practically, who had a Rice Krispies watch on her wrist and stuffed platypus squashed in her rucksack—was getting lonely, even homesick. Besides, not everything had gone according to plan for Jennifer thus far on the trip.

Razor-sharp rocks and scattered hunks of glass punctured holes in her bicycle tires, twice. The first flat came before she had even made it out of California. Days later, she was stranded again; this time a truck driver would pick her up in Lordsburg, New Mexico, and provide the sixty-mile ride to Deming, where a local man graciously repaired the bicycle tire.

JENNIFER ARRIVES IN DEMING

ON OCTOBER 16, 1991, Jennifer attended the Wednesday night service at the Deming Baptist Church, which started at 7 p.m. After the church services, Jennifer asked members of the congregation if she could sleep in the church, perhaps roll out her sleeping bag on a pew? Maybe she could pitch her tent behind the church?

Pastor Robert Summers and his wife, Loretta, offered the girl a better and safer night's rest at a fifth wheel on the couple's property nearby, where Jennifer took a warm shower and washed her hair, then watched television, before she retired to bed at approximately 10 p.m. Robert and Loretta rose early the following morning, taking Jennifer for breakfast at McDonald's at approximately 7 a.m. on October 17, and then Pastor Robert escorted her back to the church so Jennifer could retrieve her bicycle.

After parting with the Summerses, Jennifer then walked across the road with her bicycle to the Downtown Shell station and called her mother to inform her of what she had told the Summers the night before. As the fall of 1991 edged toward winter, she would bicycle for a short while in the dry, sunny land of New Mexico and then jump on a bus or flag a ride to Moorhead, Minnesota, to visit a friend who was a freshman at Concordia College.

After Lynn told her that wintertime freezes had turned the ground to iron in parts of the Midwest, Jennifer said that putting away the bicycle for a while would be a welcome scenario; fatigued and stiff from all the exercising, she was relying on Tylenol and aspirin.

"Please don't tell her that I am coming to visit," Jennifer requested of her mother. "The look on her face will be priceless."

Lynn offered to pay the bus fare from New Mexico to Minnesota. Jennifer politely reminded her mother that she still had a few hundred dollars in cash on hand and then she talked about matting and framing the poems that she had been writing at campsites and cafés, perhaps even selling them at craft fairs to earn extra money for Christmas. She floated the idea of enrolling in writing and art classes during the spring 1992 semester at the University of Montana.

"I will call you later tonight or tomorrow morning," Jennifer concluded. "I will let you know what way I'll be going to head out of New Mexico. I'm headed to Las Cruces. I'm excited to know that I'll be home for the holidays. Love you, Mom."

"I was excited that she was going to be home for Christmas," says Lynn. "When her dad was sick with leukemia, our last two Christmases were pretty sad, and they were spent at the hospital. We were hoping to have a better Christmas, and I just knew we would because she was going to be home."

Between October 1 and October 17, 1991, Jennifer called home in Missoula collect at least a dozen times. But the fourteen-minute phone call from Deming, New Mexico, would be the final time that Lynn would ever hear her daughter's voice.

"She told us that she was going to be biking to Minnesota to see her friend," Loretta Summers said in 2021. "We told her to go to Highway 70 to Interstate 40 and gave her directions to the Fair Acres Baptist Church in Las Cruces. She asked about making a cut across to Hatch. We said that that was not a good idea. There was not a lot of traffic that way, and it was not a good idea to go that way. We assumed that she went to Interstate 70. We learned later that bikes would not have been allowed on Interstate 70, so what could have happened to that poor girl?"

Thirty-years later, Jennifer Pentilla is listed on the website of the New Mexico State Police Cold Case Homicides.

WHAT HAPPENED TO JENNIFER PENTILLA?

FOLLOWING THE PHONE CALL with her mother, Jennifer Pentilla parked her white Sundance Fuji mountain bicycle against the side of the Downtown Shell station, draped her turquoise and white helmet over its handlebars, fixed her turquoise Jan Sport backpack against her shoulders, and walked inside and asked the attendant to point her toward the restroom.

According to the statement that he made to the New Mexico State Police on December 15, 1992, attendant Jesus "Chuy" Vasquez, age twenty-one, the son of the station owner, Henry Vasquez, said that Jennifer entered the business sometime at "about 10:30 (or) 10." He and Jennifer exchanged a bit of superficial chit-chat about her bicycle, "just a regular touring bike," as he recalled, "I'm pretty sure it was white." At one point he claimed that Jennifer, who, he said, was wearing "hiking boots" and "wool socks," said "something about coming from Mexicali."

"About five, ten minutes later," according to Vasquez, Jennifer exited the bathroom, made a purchase, and after departing the gas station, she ventured off, walking alongside her bike, "heading east," according to Vasquez.

"I think she was going to the travel agency," concluded Vasquez in his brief statement to Special Agent Miguel Frietzke Jr., "'cause she said something about going to the travel agency. But first she went to the phone and stayed on the phone for about ten, fifteen minutes."

Even if Jennifer used the pay phone at "about 10:30 (or) 10" after she left the Shell Station "for about ten, fifteen minutes," as Vasquez contended—Lynn's phone records substantiate the time of Jennifer's phone call to her mother at 7:52 a.m.—her conversation with Vasquez would be the last known face-to-face conversation of the teenager's life.

For the nearly 1,500-mile journey from New Mexico to Minnesota, Jennifer planned to subsist on fruit rolls, sunflower seeds, beef and cheese sticks, and peanut butter snack crackers. She was equipped with a bike repair kit, a red Swiss Army pocketknife, a pair of flashlights, lantern candles, and enamel camping cups. She would continue to take pictures along the way with her 35mm Miranda camera and purify her water whenever possible.

When her mind turned quiet and clear, she would allot time to journaling or reading from a book that her mother had sent her off with, "To My Daughter with Love on the Important Things in Life." Nighttime would be reserved for dreaming of all the things that she expected out of life, things she needed to do, and the places where she imagined she ought to go.

Jennifer, however, failed to call her mother as promised that Thursday night, failed again to call the following day, and she didn't call her mother on her birthday, October 19. October darkened into November, and November gave way to December, and one year later, some of her possessions were found forty-six miles northeast of the gas station where she was last seen, opposite Las Cruces.

ONE YEAR LATER

ON SEPTEMBER 4, 1992, Bill and Sara Soures from Farmington, New Mexico, were traveling through Hatch while on the way to visit with a family member in El Paso, Texas. While scoping out potential dove hunting spots along State Road 26, they turned down a sandy, undeveloped road across from the Las Uvas Valley Dairy. In the flat open scrub brush and among the vast fields of yucca and choya plants, no more than fifty feet from the road, Sara spotted an odd assortment of items—a couple of duffel bags stacked below a tarp—at first glance, perhaps litter between small scrubs of mesquite bushes. Probably nothing too unusual because the site was a known drinking and party spot for underage teenagers of Deming and Hatch and surrounding areas.

However, something about the mound of items seemed eerie to the couple, specifically, how the items were stacked neatly, almost as if someone were planning to come back for them, and that it was good quality camping gear that no reasonable person would simply discard.

There were backpacks, a bicycle helmet, a blue and gray tent. Moreover, at the bottom of the pile there was what appeared to be a set of handwritten journals. Full jars of baby food (not something that jibed with Jennifer's eating regimen) and cigarette butts (she certainly didn't smoke) surrounded the mound of possessions. Sara phoned the police department in Hatch to inform them about a potential crime scene.

Three days later, the couple, troubled by what to them seemed like a startling lack of interest from Hatch authorities, returned to the same spot only to find the materials stacked in the very same location. This time they gathered the possessions and took them home.

Dry and shriveled items removed from the backpacks by the Soureses were deeply private: two Bibles, one written in English, the other in Spanish; inside one, a dried, rat-chewed ten-dollar bill. There was a Blue 5 Star notebook journal with entry dates between July 11 and October 14, 1991; a tourist visa form stamped by the Mexican government that permitted entry into the country for 180 days, commencing October 5, 1991. And then a wallet containing the driver's license of a teenager from Montana skimmed across the table.

After the identification of Jennifer Pentilla was discovered among the items, the couple tracked down Jennifer's family in Montana to inform them of what had been found and to find out what had brought her to New Mexico.

TEENAGER FROM MONTANA

Jennifer Pentilla (a Finnish surname pronounced Pentell-a) was born April 4, 1973, in Butte, Montana, and came out of that place as raw—and unselfconscious about it—as the town itself. Jennifer was, by any measure, a serious girl, troubled by sometimes curious things. Even as an infant Jennifer impressed those around her as unusually intelligent and somewhat hypervigilant. It was as if her blue eyes were perpetually scanning the environment, as if they were constantly seeking information. She was also fearless, ambitious, and direct.

"She was a go-getter," says her mother, Lynn. "I knew it right away."

Her father, Nick, an army veteran and business manager, sensed it, too. Indeed, Jennifer was sitting upright at three months, crawling across the carpet with abandoned curiosity at four months, and walking steadily at eight months. She didn't want to sit still; she wasn't going to be held back.

Many of those who remember Jennifer recall a girl who projected an appealing blend of confidence and deference from the moment she walked in the door. As a teenager she was more apt to pick up a book or colored pencil or a shovel or rake than a piece of athletic equipment or accessory. She loved camping and hiking and the thrill of sleeping outdoors, which inspired her to write poems of angels and cherubs. She read Nancy Drew mysteries and studied geography, often uncannily memorizing the stats of countries she had learned about in *National Geographic* books and magazines. She liked to bake cookies and decorate the house to celebrate the change of seasons and festive occasions.

Beginning in junior high school, she began to refuse gifts around the holidays, emphasizing to her loved ones that there were people far less fortunate and thus far more deserving of such offerings than she was. Teachers frequently complimented the girl on her obvious sense of initiative, like how she'd get up extra early before school to deliver the *Great Falls Tribune*, her dog Jericho in tow; or how, as an exchange student, she worked on-site to address poverty in Africa. As a hobby, Jennifer taught herself to speak Spanish conversationally.

In October 1990, her senior year of high school, Jennifer's father, seemingly healthy until then, was stricken with heart problems and then diagnosed with leukemia. His death at age forty-four only deepened her already robust Lutheran faith.

Her sense of empathy expanded following a trip to Mexico in July 1991, where she aided the construction of water and sewer projects. Come the fall of that year, the world appeared as an ever-widening circle, where underdeveloped countries such as Mexico had "made sense," in her words, and volunteer work would be the bedrock of her entire life's course.

The promise and privilege of a long existence would not be for Jennifer Pentilla.

SUSPECT IDENTIFIED

STARTING WITH THE DISCOVERY of Jennifer's possessions in 1992, police were bombarded with phone calls from people claiming to have seen her in a variety of fantastical locations, including a pier on a wharf in San Francisco and a hippie commune outside the Grand Canyon in Arizona; other callers even suggested something more improbable: she was leading a life of deceptive anonymity in New Mexico. Statements over the years from New Mexico police officials, and available records pertaining to the Pentilla investigation, however, refute such claims of wanton vagabonding or reckless gypsying.

According to documents provided to the Pentilla family by New Mexico law enforcement, multiple witnesses reported that they saw Jesus "Chuy" Vasquez with Jennifer on the day that she was last seen, including an acquaintance named Sarah Chavez, who told law enforcement that "she saw Jennifer in the shed or a female in the shed." Another witness told New Mexico police that she had seen Jennifer with "Chuy" in a Deming store after the phone call she had made to her mother.

One document concluded with a self-evident summary sentence: "There have been several witnesses and sources that have identified Jesus "Chuy" Vasquez as the individual responsible for Jennifer's abduction and death."

On December 15, 1992, Vasquez was interviewed for the first time by law enforcement while seated in the rear of the squad car of Special Agent Miguel Frietzke Jr. of the New Mexico State Police, the conversation conducted outside the Shell gas station where Jennifer was last seen. Among glaring omissions, the questions that comprise the brief interview fail to establish the man's work schedule or what time he arrived at and departed work that day.

In September 1994, Vasquez was arrested by New Mexico State Police in a sweeping joint agency drug sale sting operation after he sold an unspecified amount of narcotics to an undercover agent. According to police reports, Vasquez, who "suffered an accidental overdose or tried to commit suicide," was "questioned about Jennifer and would not say anything."

On August 8, 1995, Deming police officer Edward Apodaca wrote to inform the Pentilla family that Chuy's ex-girlfriend Amy Chavez "saw a leather bracelet on 'Chuy' similar to Jennifer's; and when she mentioned it to him, he quit wearing it."

Apodaca said that he would continue to wait for an "anonymous letter" to appear from her killer and that he has been attempting to "befriend" Vasquez and "is still trying to get him to come clean."

Also, around that time a witness reported to New Mexico State Police seeing a "1953 Chevy truck" reverse its route and head toward a girl he saw riding a bike near the Hatch airport. The date, he said, was October 17, 1991; the girl on the bike he identified as Jennifer Pentilla. After an employee at the Quick Pick Store in Hatch told authorities that she was certain that she saw Jennifer "come in with two men, one stayed by her side, and the other stayed on the outside by the phone," New Mexico authorities announced that a farm laborer named Henry Apodaca of Hatch was "a person of interest for having bragged about abducting Jennifer." (The Quick Pick Store is located seven miles from the site where Jennifer's possessions were found.) Henry Apodaca, who died in 2011, was never charged with a crime.

On March 1, 2010, a spokesperson from the New Mexico State Police announced that the Luna County DA's office was anticipating that it would "bring charges up on a suspect" in Jennifer's case.

In October 2011, Vasquez, then forty-one, got into a fight with his brother Frank and beat him to death, eventually pleading guilty to voluntary manslaughter. The defense contended that Frank was in poor health due to a number of "undiagnosed medical conditions and extreme methamphetamine intoxication." Convinced that Frank died of a heart attack aggravated by a run-of-the-mill confrontation with his brother, the judge sentenced "Chuy" to four years in prison.

After serving his sentence, Vasquez returned to Deming, where he remained the principal subject of the investigation into Jennifer's disappearance.

On November 6, 2016, Deming officer Edward Apodaca wrote to the Pentilla family again, this time stating that he told "Chuy" repeatedly "that Jennifer deserves justice" and that he even tried to sympathize with "Chuy," allowing that Jennifer's death "might have been unintentional or even accidental." (No longer employed with the Deming Police Department, Apodaca would not comment on the Pentilla case when he was repeatedly contacted in March 2021.)

Nonetheless, authorities who have investigated Jennifer's disappearance and presumed murder leave little doubt as to conclusions they have drawn in terms of where responsibility for her absence resides.

"The guy I thought was going to get close to "Chuy" ended up going to jail," says New Mexico Police Agent Charles Boylston. "There went my way of getting any new information. I always have Jennifer in the back of my mind, and this case is very dear to my heart."

ETERNAL MEMORIES OF JENNIFER

THE SHELL SERVICE STATION is no longer in operation on Pine Street in Deming. The Sundance Fuji bike that Jennifer was riding, which has not been found, was white with green lettering; it had a front battery-operated headlight and a set of black saddle bags on the front and rear. Jennifer's aunt's name was engraved on the underside of the bike. The bike serial number was F 9101771. A leather friendship bracelet that Jennifer was wearing around the time of her disappearance has not been recovered, nor has her blue and silver sleeping bag.

The cigarette butts and jars of baby food found with Jennifer's possessions at the crime scene in Hatch are not part of the list of inventoried items said to be stored at the New Mexico State Police Crime Lab. And no evidence indicates that the latent prints on the evidence found by the Soureses were processed at a crime lab in New Mexico or Montana. The road that leads to the site of the recovery of Jennifer's possessions is blocked by a fence and locked gate, marked with a sign identifying the area as a private hunting preserve.

Before she arrived in Deming, New Mexico, in the fall of 1991, Jennifer Pentilla had changed her mind about traveling to Mexico alone and was headed toward the Midwest to visit with a friend. While she was in San Simeon, California, she mailed her mother a package that contained two heavy travel books about Mexico and her tennis shoes. Not long after Jennifer went missing, her package arrived in Missoula, creased and smudged from the trip it had taken in the girl's backpack before it was even mailed. Lynn took the unopened envelope in her hand and looked at the front. There was Jennifer's name and additional words printed there: "SOMEWHERE SOUTH."

Jennifer Pentilla would have been age forty-eight on April 4, 2021. Her birthday is a bitter occasion for her mother, another milestone that she won't celebrate with her daughter, a depressing day of emptiness and intrusive thoughts, and another gaping reminder of what it is like to raise and love a child and then have her ripped away.

"Jennifer is daily on my mind," says Lynn. "But come April and October, my mind is consumed with thoughts as to what happened to my sweet, beautiful eighteen-year-old daughter, and it haunts me that no one has been able to find her. Why has the person who took Jennifer away from her family in Montana not been caught yet? Why do they get to go on living as if nothing happened? I can't help but wonder who else this person has hurt in their lifetime?"

JODY FERN HOWARD

VANISHED: OCTOBER 7, 1991
VANISHED FROM: WOLF POINT

SHE WAS TWENTY-EIGHT YEARS OLD and lived in Frazer, within the Fort Peck Indian Reservation. She had four children, with eight years separating the youngest from the oldest. She had three brothers and a sister, all of whom lived within six blocks. The disappearance of Jody Howard, a member of the Fort Peck Assiniboine and Sioux tribes, is one of the many dozens of unsolved missing person cases in Montana involving indigenous women, several of which have been the subject of film and television treatments.

Not one of the high-profile cases, very little is known about Howard and her life. One of her brothers later told investigators that her upbringing was harsh, and that she was "trapped in a nightmare," he said. Since the age of nine, a dark cloud of sexual abuse at the hands of an adult had hung over her childhood. At eighteen, Howard set out on her own. She worked as a receptionist and cleaned motels in Missoula, hoping to attend college. Education would not be her ticket out of abuse. She didn't have the money to enroll in classes. She worked multiple low-wage jobs. In her private life, she was drawn to ruffians and rowdy, rebellious types. She ended up meeting a man who had roots in the Wolf Point area, too. She soon became pregnant, and the baby was born in Wolf Point. Several more children came in rapid succession.

According to her family, Jody was an outgoing, friendly person. One of her brothers characterized Jody's personality by saying, "She greeted everyone she knew." Whoever the last person was to greet her on October 7, 1991, presumably ended her life.

DETAILS OF DISAPPEARANCE LIMITED

THERE IS PRECIOUS little information about what Jody did on the day she disappeared. She was last seen at the Town Pump gas station in Wolf Point, Montana, on October 7, 1991, and when she left there, no one heard from her again. At the Town Pump, she purchased a pack of cigarettes and a few snacks, and she made small talk with the clerk, a relative of one of her friends. She didn't drive to the gas station in her own vehicle. She told the clerk that she was waiting on a friend. She had red polish on her toenails, and her blue pajamas were too big for her.

Her family later indicated that it was unlike Jody to go long stretches without contacting them. One of her aunts told a tribal publication that she was in contact with Jody regularly and that she visited with her at least every other day. Despite that assertion, her family did not report Jody missing until November 10, 1991, more than a month after she disappeared.

Posters distributed within tribal boundaries show a picture of Jody and bold, black vital statistics: twenty-eight-year-old Native American woman; five feet, four inches tall; and approximately 125 pounds. Below the photo, the poster notes that "she had black hair, brown eyes, very white teeth, and two distinguishing marks," listing a tattoo on one of the fingers of her left hand and a birthmark on the right side of her neck.

According to one tribal newspaper report from 1994, Nelson Heart, the investigator originally assigned to the case on behalf of the Bureau of Indian Affairs, thought foul play may have been involved because the funds in Jody's tribal bank account had not been touched in the three years since her disappearance.

For many years after she went missing, law enforcement officials received several reports of sightings of Jody near her hometown and in surrounding states, but none of the tips led them to Jody. Someone said that she might have been living in Lethbridge, Canada. Montana investigators were dispatched in every direction and ultimately shot down and debunked each and every rumor.

"We've just been looking all over," Heart said to one local television outlet on the anniversary of the woman's disappearance. "You can't make someone appear out of the air. We live in a land that's hard to find people."

In 1995, approximately four years after Jody's disappearance, law enforcement officials decided to examine the validity of a rumor that had been circulating in the community that Jody had been murdered and dumped into the Brockton lagoon near Poplar, Montana. Officials drained the lagoon and searched for Jody's remains, but they did not find anything.

The case of Jody Fern Howard stands in a similar place today to where it stood decades ago: vanished and unsolved. No leads. No suspects. No body. Little chance of resolution.

JOHN REAMER

VANISHED: MARCH 27, 1994
VANISHED FROM: HELENA

John Reamer's girlfriend dropped him off at his apartment on Wilder Street in Helena. It was late March. The sun was shining on the same drab scene it illuminated every other morning at eleven o'clock. Darcy Kamerman commented on the grayness, and Reamer nodded. They had spent the sunless weekend with their young son at Darcy's mother's residence in Three Forks. The relationship was platonic; she had long soured on Reamer's ability to be a good partner.

"End of the line, Big John," Darcy quipped.

"Sure thing," replied Reamer.

According to published and previously unpublished police reports, Darcy noticed a car she didn't know parked in front at Reamer's apartment. The car was smashed up in front, had a bashed-in grill, and the back window was badly cracked.

Inside Reamer's place, she noticed the silhouette of a body, a tall, lanky frame of a man. She assumed Reamer knew the person who was there, perhaps an acquaintance from the video rental store where he often rented Nintendo games. Reamer could burn away hours playing Mike Tyson's Punch-out and Blades of Steel.

Apprehensive, she walked him to the front door and stayed for about ten minutes. Reamer did not introduce the man, who went to the refrigerator and opened two cans of the

Schlitz he had brought. While the man fidgeted with some
magazines on the kitchen table and sucked down his beer,
Reamer turned on the television and watched it, though
slumped a little more heavily than usual in his armchair.

She never asked for the stranger's name. Reamer stared
transfixed at the professional wrestling match on the television, and the stranger mumbled something incoherently
about how that afternoon he had been drinking beer on a
public highway.

The next morning, before Reamer left for his classes at Carroll College, he spoke to Darcy Kamerman and her mother,
Sandy Kamerman. He said nothing unusual. He wasn't especially talkative. He wasn't guarded. The last thing he said was
that he was going to the bedroom to button his shirt and that
the shirt had sand in the pocket from Canyon Ferry.

He was never heard from again.

REAMER REPORTED MISSING

DARCY WAS UNABLE to reach him for several days and asked
a friend to check on him. On April 4, 1994, after the friend
could not get an answer at Reamer's apartment, the Kamer-
mans began contacting members of Reamer's family—cousins, aunts, uncles—and his friends to find out whether they
had heard from him. Sandy then reported Reamer missing to
Bozeman police (since she lived in Three Forks) while one of
Reamer's friends from Carroll College informed authorities
in Helena.

That same evening Darcy and Sandy Kamerman checked
Reamer's apartment. They found his personal items, including his schoolbooks and wallet. Dishes were stacked in the
kitchen sink. Two coffee mugs were still on the drain board,

and the remains of the coffee grounds lingered in the drain. His car was parked outside the residence. His favorite cowboy hat could not be found, however; he may have been wearing it. Nothing appeared to be out of place in the apartment, and there were no signs of struggle. His billfold was on the dresser, and other textbooks were stacked on the bed, along with his backpack.

Did John Reamer walk away from a life that had grown increasingly inimical and succumb to mental illness, or was his fate somehow linked to the unexplained stranger who he was last seen with at his apartment?

DARK STRAIN OF REAMER

AN AMATEUR KICKBOXER, John Reamer received a felony assault conviction stemming from a fight at the Jester's Bar in Helena in 1992. He received a six-year deferred sentence for the crime and was ordered into chemical dependency treatment. In 1993, his probation officer recommended that the sentence be reinstated because Reamer had failed to complete his treatment and had been arrested twice for driving while under the influence. When he disappeared, Reamer was in criminal jeopardy, potentially facing more prison time because of the second drunk-driving arrest—he had spent thirty days in lockup after the first arrest. This time the sentence could be longer once these violations of his probation conditions were factored in.

Brown-haired and brown-eyed, an enrolled member of the Makah Indian Nation—he sported a red, yellow, and green tattoo of a Makah design on his upper right arm, a circular tribal silhouette with two feathers hanging down—Reamer was in his twenties and a new father.

He had a dark strain in his character. In fact, Kamerman gave birth to Reamer's son while Reamer was behind bars. Reamer wrote frequently to Darcy and Sandy Kamerman while he was incarcerated, declaring that he would get his life together and whip his chemical dependency so he could have a relationship with his son.

"I still have all of the times that he wrote his letters," said Sandy Kamerman. "The letters were always cordial and optimistic, and the later ones evolved into an expression of real faith. I brought my grandson to visit him at the jail. I walked in the jail, and the baby started crying and put his hand on the glass and started saying the word daddy. That was the first time that John had seen him. He was released, and he continued to keep a relationship with his son."

For the duration of Reamer's incarceration, Sandy Kamerman acted as his spiritual guide, and on some parallels, his mother. Abandoned by his own mother at the age of six, Reamer knew little about her, except that she drank hard and was in jail for resisting arrest just one month after he was born. John called Sandy "Mom." One card Reamer sent to her before his disappearance thanked her for showing him what love is all about.

After he was released from jail, Reamer decided to pursue a college education, and he moved to Helena to enroll in Carroll College. He found work for a contractor and seemed like he had discovered purpose in his life. While Reamer didn't rekindle a romantic relationship with Darcy, he frequently traveled to Three Forks to visit with Darcy and Sandy Kamerman and his son.

He was facing a tedious uphill pull from the minute he left the penitentiary. Yes, he was doing better, making the adjustments to establish a new path. On the other hand, he was losing his ongoing battle against chemical dependency and bipolar disorder.

"He'd been suicidal in the past," said Sandy Kamerman. "He had been prescribed medication to control his conditions, but he wasn't taking it at the time he went missing."

Police reports indicate that friends of Reamer's saw him as persistently melancholy and the person who arrived at a party only days before the disappearance was desperately unhappy, fragile, and belligerent. A neighbor said that he'd sometimes knock on their door at 10 p.m., saying he felt anxious, and insist on sleeping over. Friends and acquaintances of Reamer's said that he loathed his life. He loathed the country. Helena bored him. There was nothing to do. He had no friends at college, and he despised the locals his age (he longed to return to the Makah Indian Reservation in Washington State), who were interested only in motorcycles, drugs, drinking, pornography, and hanging around with the flotsam of Helena in seedy dives such as the Jester's Bar.

One friend told police that Reamer was "fine when he was taking his prescription medications" and speculated that he might have stopped taking them and slipped back into "the drug culture" or "the drug den."

No tangible proof exists of either scenario, although according to Sandy Kamerman, Reamer called his sister to ask for money and wouldn't tell her what it was for; and the fact that he kept a hatchet hanging near his bed led her to believe he might be associating with some unsavory characters. Reamer also was known to sink into a miserable state of depression, the worst of which resulted in threats of suicide. Sometimes he'd adopt an alias and claim that his last name was Hanson or Parchman or Phillips.

"He never followed through with the suicidal threats, and he seemed to be making progress in coping with all of his emotions," said Sandy Kamerman. "From Christmastime in 1993 until his disappearance, he was the most stable and happy as I had ever seen him."

Nonetheless, Kamerman said that the last time she saw Reamer on a visit to Three Forks, he made his farewell sound permanent. That visit in March 1994 was the last time she saw him and still clings to the memories of the barbed, tender, despairing bond between grandmother and the father of her first grandchild.

"His final words were, 'I love you,'" said Kamerman.

INDOMITABLE NATURE OF HOPE

AT SIXTY-SIX, Sandy Kamerman keeps boxes of Reamer's personal items—a fishing bag and rod; a weathered, brown leather jacket; a white tank top; a small basket he wove as a child, and miscellaneous photographs—at her home in Three Forks, in the event that Reamer comes back. Perhaps incredulously, Kamerman said that she still believes that he is still alive. In her version of events, somebody was after his life the night of March 27, 1994. She speculated that the threat was probably related to the "bad drug culture."

"I do think he left before they got him and that he escaped the people who were coming for him," said Sandy. "There's no proof of this, just a gut feeling."

The first few years after Reamer disappeared, Kamerman said that she would occasionally receive weird hang-up calls, usually in the nighttime, or see strange cars drive slowly past her house along the gravel road, and other family members reported being tailed or cornered by unfamiliar vehicles.

Kamerman said that, though he was deeply troubled, Reamer had "a kind, compassionate demeanor" and "soft heart" and that perhaps he had cleaned himself up and was alive in 2023 and maybe even working with people battling addiction.

Reamer was under state supervision at the time of his disappearance for probation violations, so, theoretically, he could be charged with absconding and technically remains a fugitive from justice. But it seems unlikely that he will reemerge from the shadows one clear, sunny morning and turn himself over to the authorities.

FIRST RESPONSE OF POLICE:
REAMER SKIPPED TOWN

AT THE TIME of his disappearance, police in Helena issued a bulletin to the news media that indicated that he had simply skipped town. It wasn't treated as a homicide or foul play situation, said one of the police detectives who later handled the case. "There was absolutely no sign of him," Captain Wes Leyritz said. "It seemed like he beat a fast trail and fast break out of town."

Reamer's case is reopened every few years, and police have interviewed and reinterviewed all his friends, family, and acquaintances. Leyritz said that police long ago visited the video rental store Reamer frequented and attempted to obtain information about the man Kamerman saw the morning of his disappearance but were never able to ascertain his identity. Police pulled phone records and said that Reamer made a number of phone calls to fishing companies in Alaska shortly before his disappearance; he had worked there prior to moving to Montana. But the calls never provided the investigation with any real clues.

Although the Helena police have compiled a list of "persons of interest," the investigation lacks a solid suspect or motive.

The case file has been handed from one detective to another over the years, and the sense within the department is that no detective could do the case further justice. According to Detective Danny Davis, Reamer's case is still being "actively investigated" and though it remains as cold as a mackerel, he said that he owed it to the man's family to continue to probe. His belief is that Reamer didn't vanish of his own accord, and "someone somewhere knows where he is." He added that the police are not any closer to solving the case in 2023 than they were when Reamer was first reported missing in 1994.

"As an optimist, you always maintain hope that that could change," said Davis. "There haven't been any active or actionable leads for some time now. As an investigator, you want to see this thing resolved."

JULIANNE STALLMAN

MURDERED: NOVEMBER 29, 1994
MURDER LOCATION: BUTTE

On Tuesday, November 29, 1994, forty-one-year-old Julianne Stallman was murdered in her home at approximately 3:30 p.m., the result of multiple stab wounds of the chest and incised and stab wounds of the neck and blunt force trauma to the head. Butte–Silver Bow Coroner Dan Hollis described an especially vicious set of circumstances in his forty-four-page autopsy report.

The crime scene at 1028 California Avenue was distinctly inhumane. The sofa in the living room was splashed with blood. The carpet was such a bloody mess in some heavily saturated spots that it had collected enough to form mini puddles. There seemed to be no real motive, other than pure hatred, which could have been the most compelling motive of all. No money was gained.

On Wednesday, November 30, police looked for leads and Butte–Silver Bow Chief of Detectives John Walsh and his investigators interviewed a number of people, including relatives, neighbors, and friends of the victim. Not a single neighborhood resident reported seeing anything out of the ordinary at Stallman's house. It wasn't the kind of neighborhood where residents were fastidious about locking their doors.

In 1991, Julianne had bought the modest place—her very first house—a one-level structure originally built in 1904. She

On Tuesday, November 29, 1994, forty-one-year-old Julianne Stallman was murdered in her home in Butte at approximately 3:30 p.m.,the result of multiple stab wounds to the chest, incised and stab wounds to the neck, and blunt-force trauma to the head. Police identified a pair of suspects known to the victim, but they were unable to make any arrests in the case. COURTESY JENNIFER MACPHEE

had moved quite a bit in her life, and she was overjoyed to have something of her own now. She painted it and decorated it and fixed it up as nicely as she could afford. Sometimes she would stand on her lawn, in the bright noon sun, and smile. Owning the house made her beam.

Julianne's granddaughter was born in May 1991, and both her daughter, Jennifer, and her granddaughter moved in with Julianne when the baby was just a few months old. But they had moved out months before her death. Julianne's son, John Stallman, twenty-two, lived with his mother at the time of the murder.

She was a waitress at Jacalyn's restaurant, 3502 Harrison. Her regular days off were Sunday and Monday. People close to her called her "Julie." Just a few days before she was murdered, she had hosted Thanksgiving at her house. Guests included Julianne's children; her daughter Jennifer's two young children; and her on-again, off-again boyfriend, Brian Skinner, and his son. Skinner, attracted to her girlish spirit and sense of humor, at first had treated her decently.

The Sunday before her death, Julianne had put up all her Christmas decorations. The following day she spent preparing for Christmas at her mother's. "Sunday (Mom) put all of her Christmas stuff (out)," said her daughter Jennifer MacPhee. "Her tree went all out. She loved Christmas. Decorations were up on the day that she died."

The last known contact Stallman had with anyone was between 3 and 3:15 p.m., a telephone conversation with her sister, allowing investigators to speculate that Stallman was killed between 3:15 and 4 p.m. Jennifer called the house at 3:30 p.m., and there was no response.

John Stallman found his mother's body at about 6 p.m. John said that he used a key to get into the house, but he did not know if the door was locked. He called Jennifer at about 6:30 p.m. to tell her their mother was dead.

VIOLENT DEATH SHOCKS BUTTE

THERE WERE NO immediate signs of a robbery or any other crime, except for the murder itself. There also was no evidence of forced entry at the house. The snow was no more than a film underfoot, like thin white wool drawn across the street and sidewalk. Still, fresh impressions of several pairs of boot and shoe prints led to the front porch. None were located in the back or below any of the windows or around the cellar.

Stallman's violent death shocked and haunted the neighborhood, and the crime left lingering fear and suspicion in the usually quiet and safe area. Terrified neighbors were losing sleep. Some would only speak with reporters through latched screen doors. Parents started walking their teenage daughters to and from school. Unescorted kids formed groups to ensure their own sense of well-being.

In a press release, Butte–Silver Bow County Sheriff John McPherson told Butte residents that they should not be worried. There is "no danger to the community," McPherson wrote. At a press conference later that evening, McPherson told the media that it appeared as if Stallman's house was not broken into, and that she was personally targeted, the unfortunate victim of a vicious domestic crime.

"Because of the violent, intimate nature of the death—the amount of overkill, the slashing of the neck, so many stab wounds—from the beginning we have felt like it was someone who knew Julianne," one Butte detective familiar with the case said in 2023. "It was so hateful and brutal, and it's hard to believe that it was someone that we are not familiar with."

MURDER OF A QUIET, BEAUTIFUL WOMAN

JULIANNE WAS ONE of seven children, the third oldest, raised in a small house at 107 South Alabama. She went to Butte High and Central High and twirled batons as a majorette. She was a candy striper at the hospital and wrote poems while she was in high school. She didn't travel too far from Butte, other than family visits, and didn't own a passport. She worked at the truck stop diner as a waitress. For a few years she moved to a cabin along the Wise River, to be close to one of her sisters.

Most residents who publicly discussed Stallman said that she was "a quiet neighbor," and even those who conceded that they didn't really know her said that she was "beautiful" and "radiated charm."

"She was happy," said her daughter, Jennifer MacPhee. "She was a lover, not a fighter. She didn't like conflict. She was always smiling. She had an infectious, beautiful laugh. She had a sweet little voice. She could knit or crotchet or cross-stitch anything. She loved people and was friendly and polite and generous with her time and herself and her energy. She was a great human and a joy to be around."

DAUGHTER DEMANDS ANSWERS; NONE EVER PROVIDED

THREE MONTHS LATER, the stabbing death remained unsolved, and her daughter was at her wit's end. She demanded answers and ratcheted up the intensity and frequency of her pleas.

Jennifer continued to probe and ask questions and at times beg the Sheriff's Office to release more details, and to vigilantly

Since her mother's grisly death, Julianne Stallman's daughter, Jennifer MacPhee, has pushed as hard as she could for comeuppance, motivated by the strongest sense of homage. "My mother would have pushed and done things a thousand times harder than I ever have," said MacPhee. "She loved me with her entire being, and I know that. She would have fought for me, and I'm fighting for her. She deserves peace, and so does everyone who loved her." COURTESY JENNIFER MACPHEE check every single tip, rumor, lead, or innuendo. She called the local newspapers and told them she was concerned about a lack of progress in the investigation. Several friends of Jennifer's began calling the newspapers and radio stations and voicing similar concerns. Every two weeks, she would call and remind the *Montana Standard* of the unsolved murder that needed the public's grave attention and that any story that they could whip together would be better than no story at all.

"I felt as if the community had put the murder at the wayside," Jennifer MacPhee said in 2023. "The person who murdered my mother was out there somewhere, and it was frustrating because it seemed like nobody cared. In the beginning, the Butte police said that they would come by weekly to visit. But they came a few times and stopped. The sheriff occasionally visited my grandparents. I had a personality conflict with two of the detectives, and the more I raised a fuss, the less they responded to me."

DAY OF THE MURDER

ACCORDING TO published police reports and the accounts of Julianne's family and friends, on the evening of the murder, it appeared as if Stallman was cooking soup—a portion consistent with a party of one—when she was killed. Julianne was a neat, tidy person, but cupboards were open and items haphazardly arranged that shouldn't have been. Perhaps the murderer came in through the front door, which, it was reported, "was never locked except at night." Perhaps the murderer brought the weapon. There was a violent struggle; blood was found in various rooms. "We know that she definitely put up a fight," said MacPhee.

POLICE CONFIDENT SHE KNEW HER KILLER

JULIANNE'S SON, JOHN, was considered the police's first suspect. But after digging, the investigators couldn't find anything that he had said or done to sustain their suspicions.

"Everything he said shook out," said one Butte investigator in 2023. "Believe me, we shook. Nothing doing there."

But the Butte–Silver Bow County Police did release the names of their three top suspects and even publicly identified two "persons of interest," people who they believed knew more about the homicide than they had told investigators. The suspects: Brian Skinner and Van Stallman. The persons of interest, female acquaintances of Skinner and Van Stallman: Jaime LeProwse (Skinner) and Sharon Stoner (Van Stallman).

Matt Pyatt was also named as a suspect early in the investigation by Butte authorities. Pyatt had been implicated by Dillon authorities in the murder of Judy Focher years earlier. In the early 2000s, Jennifer received a troubling phone call from Norm Focher, Judy's husband, and she said that he believed that similarities existed in the two murders too coincidental to ignore.

"Norm Focher found me and called me on a landline," said MacPhee. "He described how Judy had been kidnapped and found dead six weeks later in Big Hole. He said that her head was ran over. He said that Matt lived in Big Hole and so did my mom. Judy looked similar to my mom. He said that Matt had been identified as a suspect in the case. I'd met Matt as a teenager. He was at the club. She may have spent the night at his cabin once. They'd float the river together."

All available records related to the Stallman murder singling out Matt Pyatt have been solidly redacted. An officer close to the case, who requested not to be identified, said that Pyatt was on "the short list of real serious suspects" but he has since been "cleared."

"Years later, we got his DNA off a piece of chewing gum and a bottle or something, and it didn't match," said the officer. "He wasn't our guy."

SUSPECT BRIAN SKINNER SPEAKS

SKINNER FINALLY SPOKE OPENLY about the accusation several years ago, when he appeared on a television program about the murder, and he admitted that he was one of the only "logical suspects, I guess," though he denied committing the murder.

The program was filmed in Butte, and Jennifer MacPhee traveled from South Dakota to participate in the event. She did not know that Skinner was going to be a part of the production until the day of her interview. Skinner traveled from Idaho to Butte, and both he and MacPhee were put up in hotels just a few blocks apart. After their interviews, the two—the suspect and the victim's daughter—met at a café in Butte and talked for approximately two hours.

"I was always on the fence as to whether or not he did it," said MacPhee. "After you see the show, it definitely seems like he is the prime suspect. Maybe he knows something. He answers all of the questions in a guilty manner."

At one point, Skinner is asked by the interviewer to explain how and why his DNA was located at the Stallman house, with significant quantities traced and pinpointed in the kitchen sink, drain, and floor. He said that he would come over to the house to fix things, and before the murder he had put up Julianne's kitchen cabinets and had cut himself badly.

He also talked about the Thanksgiving dinner days earlier at Julianne's house and described in crystal-clear detail the knife that he had used to cut the turkey.

Skinner's response to this question in particular raised her antennae.

"He would never hang out at my mom's house," said MacPhee. "When they were dating, they would spend the evenings at his house. They dated for four years, and for him to come to my mom's house was rare. He talked about doing something with the kitchen cabinets and cutting himself and that there might have been blood on the wall there. He never said anything like that before to anyone, ever."

In the interview, Skinner boasts about how he "had a lot of women back in those days," and he was "pissed off" that Julianne was seeing Van Stallman.

SECOND SUSPECT: VAN STALLMAN

JULIANNE WAS MARRIED to Van Stallman for several years, and the couple had divorced about three years before the murder. Van Stallman's sole interview with police is a matter of public record. It consists of no more than six pages and could be read from start to finish in about twelve minutes. It is conspicuous for its noticeable lack of hard questions or follow-up inquiries. In the interview, Van places himself in Butte on the Monday after his ex-wife was murdered and said that he "didn't remember what time" he had arrived in Butte one day before.

MacPhee said that she never wanted to believe that someone that she loved—her stepfather, who she had a relatively solid relationship with—could be responsible for such a sick, vicious act. Van died in December 2016.

"I had seen Van from time to time after my mother was killed," said MacPhee. "But when he refused to take a polygraph test, it was then that I cut ties with him. When he had cancer, I thought, Van, please leave a dying declaration, and there was none of that. My mom's sister spent a lot of time with him before he died—and there was no dying declaration. When I first asked him to do a polygraph, it was a hard no. He was very adamant that he wouldn't. There I was begging someone I loved as a stepfather to take the polygraph test. And when Van's wife [Sharon Stoner] died, there was no dying declaration, either. As far as outed suspects, that leaves Brian Skinner and his wife, Jaime LeProwse."

The true crime program that featured the Stallman murder helped push an awareness of the murder to a national level and led to processing some of the evidence in storage in Butte at the Montana State Crime Laboratory. The results, however, were convoluted.

"There was an unknown male DNA profile found on a throw rug in front of the sink and on a towel hung from the bedroom door," said Dane Byers, a forensics examiner at the Montana State Crime Lab. "Those two profiles matched. But it's uncertain if that was a suspect. The DNA came from a mixture. We found unknown male DNA on the victim's pants and jeans and one of her shoes. That, too, is unknown [whether it came from the suspect], and it's also a mixture. Most cases are closed through DNA usually coming from a single source sample. Cases have been solved using a mixture sample.

"There was not a good enough sample to separate, and that means we are testing and retesting. We are sequencing it out more. Right now, it's not eligible to be entered into the DNA databases. But that's always evolving, and that keeps us going. If even the person is dead—we don't need to know—just the who."

Jennifer MacPhee said that she still retains a slight glimmer of hope that the murder of her mother will be solved. Over the years, she has tried to not become too embittered and to not believe that the Butte police botched the investigation. Still, the frustration she feels toward the investigators and how they've handled—or mishandled—the case often rises to the surface.

"There was missing and misplaced evidence and evidence that was never tested and never left Butte," said MacPhee. "Five years ago, a knife was finally tested, but the DNA was too degraded to figure out a profile. The case has switched hands over the years many times, and any time there is a new detective, I give them time to look over the case, and none of them ever seemed to have read the case file. I've never thrown the Butte police under the bus for incompetence. I've never wanted to bite the hand that might feed me. But it is never going to feed me."

DAUGHTER FIGHTS FOR JUSTICE

AT ONE O'CLOCK on December 3, 1994, a public memorial service was conducted for Julianne Stallman. Despite the bitter cold, nearly three hundred friends and neighbors attended. Two violins, a cello, a harp, and eight voices provided music from the church balcony. The thirty-five-minute service concluded with the "Hallelujah Chorus" from Handel's *Messiah* as the casket was carried down the aisle into the stark, snowy afternoon.

Since her mother's grisly death, MacPhee has pushed as hard as she could for comeuppance, and she said she isn't motivated to find justice because it would allow her to self-heal or find some semblance of elusive peace; she's motivated by the strongest sense of homage.

"My mother would have pushed and done things a thousand times harder than I ever have," said MacPhee. "She loved me with her entire being, and I know that. She would have fought for me, and I'm fighting for her. She deserves peace, and so does everyone who loved her."

CLIFFORD NELSON

MURDERED: SEPTEMBER 30, 1996

MURDER LOCATION: SEELEY LAKE

IN THE EARLY MORNING HOURS of Monday, September 30, 1996, Clifford Lee Nelson was murdered by gunfire in his home in Seeley Lake. At least one intruder barged into the forty-eight-year-old man's residence and pumped him full of bullets in his own bedroom.

Clifford lived in what one friend described as "a luxurious tourist cabin of the mid-90s," with a thick carpet and wood-paneled walls and everything from cellophane-sealed shoe rags to three big televisions. It had a distinct smell of evergreen and holly and was the setting of many wine and fruitcake parties. He was found barefoot, a few short steps from the bathroom in the bedroom corner, face down in a red puddle.

Nelson was a highly respected teacher and member of the community. He had been named Teacher of the Year for the State of Montana for 1981. He had taught math, social studies, English, history, and drama to seventh and eighth graders at Seeley Lake Elementary School, where he also coached track and field and baseball. Students were variously quoted in a number of newspapers calling Nelson "dedicated," "generous," and "inspiring." Patience, they said, was one of his hallmarks. In November, he would have celebrated his twenty-year anniversary on the job.

Nelson was also a career seasonal ranger in Montana parks, having worked as an interpreter at Little Bighorn National Battlefield since the late 1960s. Nothing about the job ever seemed dull or unimportant to him.

Detectives investigating the murder of Nelson determined that he was killed by birdshot from a 12-gauge shotgun, and that on the same evening two 12-gauge shotgun blasts were also fired at the high school where he taught. Two locals, both former students and both of whom had had problems with Nelson when they were in junior high school, quickly became suspects in the case.

Police learned that the two had been drinking heavily on the night of the murder—brandy, Jägermeister, rum, vodka, cheap merlot, you name it—and were seen in the area of his home. Witnesses said that they weren't in an especially good mood that night, and the more they drank, the darker, the gloomier they became. More bottles of wine, beer, and whisky were passed about. The men lit cigarettes and smoked in sullen silence. They rolled thick blunts of marijuana.

At first, authorities had only a circumstantial case, with little physical evidence to tie the two young men to the crime scene. As Missoula County police detectives slowly tried to build a case against the former students, the town mourned the loss of a great educator, mentor, friend, and neighbor.

LAID TO REST

Raised on a farm in Forman, North Dakota, Nelson was the seventh of eight children and the only college graduate among his siblings. In addition to family and friends from North Dakota, hundreds of others attended a town-wide memorial service at Seeley Lake. As an expression of the community's grief, a scholarship was quickly established in his name.

"Everyone in Seeley Lake came out—a thousand or more people," said Jeff Briggs, one of Nelson's former students. "The entire town loved Coach Nelson. There wasn't a person in the town who didn't come out from the entire town. The entire town was there, except two."

Described in his obituary as "a devout Christian," he was buried near his childhood home in Forman after a funeral service at the town's Trinity Lutheran Church. Predeceased by his father, his survivors at the time of his death included his mother, three brothers, four sisters, and numerous nieces and nephews.

FORMER STUDENTS CHARGED

SOON, SHERIFF'S DEPUTIES arrested "Rambo" Hooser, nineteen, and Matt Livingston, twenty-one, of Seeley Lake for the slaying of Nelson. They were charged with the homicide and with the shooting at Seeley Lake High School and ordered to be held on $500,000 bond. Both a 12-gauge shotgun and a nickel-plated, brass-lined .38 revolver were seized from Livingston's Toyota 4Runner. The serial number of the .38 had been defaced.

An informant told investigators that Hooser had threatened to kill Nelson. Hooser, a logger, had been expelled from Seeley Lake Elementary School years earlier after a conflict with Nelson and subsequently failed to graduate from high school. He blamed Nelson for his plight. According to the informant, Hooser got drunk frequently and when he did, he railed against Nelson and sometimes he would get "too depressed to talk."

According to police reports, Hooser was the ringleader of a group of troubled delinquents, and his parents groused to neighbors and friends about what they saw as stubbornness and self-absorption. His mother described him as an "unexploded bomb." Livingston, though the older of the two, was reported to have been under Hooser's yoke.

DEFENDANTS ACQUITTED

"RAMBO" HOOSER was put on trial first, and the prosecution's case was marked by largely circumstantial evidence and little solid physical evidence connecting him to the murder. It was established that Hooser had a vendetta against Nelson and was harboring a grudge against him, but the prosecution had a difficult time placing him at the scene of the murder. Precious little forensic evidence tied Hooser to the homicide, and the defense pointed to a host of other scenarios, including two other former students of Nelson's as the possible culprits. The defense steered clear of mentioning or even alluding to the codefendant.

On May 30, 1996, the jury in the trial of Hooser found him not guilty. The jury foreman, according to the *Missoulian*, felt the case against Hooser "wasn't proved beyond a reasonable doubt." The foreman was quoted as saying, "We felt that there were a number of people who could have done it. . . . We just had far too many doubts for a conviction."

The acquittal of Hooser for all intents and purposes ended the possibility of the trial of Matt Livingston. Immediately, the county attorney moved for dismissal based on the negative outcome of the Hooser debacle.

The Cold Case Squad at the Missoula County Sheriff's Office is actively searching for new information in the case, hoping that intimate knowledge of the crime still resides not too far from where it happened.

"Seeley Lake was a very small, tight-knit community then, and it is still a very tight-knit community today," said David Conway, a Missoula County detective. "Many of the people who were involved, they grew up there and they grew up together as friends. What we hope all these years later is that with so much time that has passed, someone has had a change of attitude or a change of heart. Someone who may know something we hope will come forward and give us a more truthful statement than has been done in the past. The truth is still possible to learn."

Conway added that Nelson's memory is as sterling today as it was when he was living. Most of his students adored him, and his coworkers at the school called him a paragon of good teaching.

"The crime still shocks the community, even now, because he was such a popular educator and pillar," said Conway.

ANGELA MARIE BROWN

MURDERED: OCTOBER 15, 1997
MURDER LOCATION: LIVINGSTON

ONE EARLY MORNING in February 1998, two fishermen found a badly decomposed body in the Yellowstone River, about ten miles east of Livingston.

The body was sent to the state crime lab in Missoula and identified on February 9, 1998, as Angela Marie Brown. Park County Sheriff Charley Johnson had a hunch it was Angela—and he was right. The body was released to her family. But, according to Johnson, her family was heavily suspected to be complicit in the woman's death.

"From the time of the discovery of the body, there was no way to think that it was anything other than a criminal case and a homicide case," said Johnson in 2023. "You had to consider the abrupt disappearance, the nature of what Angela was involved in and her life, and the kind of people that she called her friends. Her family wasn't much better than her friends. They were probably much worse."

SOCIAL AUTOPSY OF ANGELA

DECEMBER 14, 1964, Brown was born in Coeur d'Alene, Idaho, and moved with her family to Park County when she was six years old. In her mid-twenties, Brown got caught up in the drug lifestyle and fell into a relationship with a man

IN MEMORY OF
ANGELA MARIE BROWN
December 14, 1964 — October, 1997

After spending the morning with her mother, Angela Brown disappeared suddenly on October 15, 1997. The thirty-three-year-old left behind her car, some money, and most importantly, two children, Kristin and Destiny. One early morning in February 1998, two fishermen found her badly decomposed body in the Yellowstone River, about ten miles east of Livingston.

who was struggling with serious mental health and substance abuse issues. Brown became pregnant—twice. The couple tried to work out their problems in therapy, but the relationship was doomed. An ugly custody dispute ensued, filled with restraining orders and accusations of domestic violence on both sides. Eventually, the man relinquished his parental rights and skipped town. Brown was in and out of rehab facilities, though she was considered a loving, compassionate mother, at least when she was straight.

At thirty-one, she moved on to harder drugs. The following year, she moved in with her mother in Livingston and after an arrest for simple possession of marijuana, turned against the drug culture. In fact, she even agreed to work with law enforcement in several sting operations intended to put away low- and mid-level street dealers in Park County and their bigger suppliers elsewhere in Montana.

In the fall of 1997, Brown had just recovered from a long-term methamphetamine habit. She filed an application at the local job corps and was keen to start work. She started to get reacquainted with some old friends, people outside of the drug culture, people who were better adjusted, people who might become positive influences, and provide the right healing ties. She was hoping to move with her children into their own place, close to where the three of them now lived with her mother. After nearly a decade of heartache and hard luck, all seemed to be going right in Brown's world. Over the years she had made her bed hard; if it hurt lying on it, she didn't complain.

"She was changing and growing and doing better," said an uncle of Angela's who requested anonymity. "It's really fucking sad what they all done to her, for nothing."

SUDDEN DISAPPEARANCE
AND GRISLY DISCOVERY

AFTER SPENDING THE MORNING with her mother, Brown disappeared suddenly on October 15, 1997. She left behind her car, some money, and, most importantly, two children, Kristin and Destiny. According to her brothers, she told them that she was planning to run some quick errands. Two days later, one of them phoned the police. Her aunt, Sally Miller, spearheaded efforts to find Angela.

Four months after she was reported missing, two fishermen found her corpse stuck in the reeds of a slow-moving tributary off the Yellowstone River. From there it was shipped to the crime lab in Missoula and identified.

In subsequent years, Sheriff Johnson didn't say too much about the case, wouldn't disclose any new information, and deferred media inquiries to Park County Coroner Albert Jenkins.

"I wanted to make sure that all of the bad actors and key players weren't tipped off," said Johnson. "And there are some bad actors, really. We damn well knew who they were, and we still do. But nothing will ever be done about it. It's too late. I hope I'm wrong."

The targets of the investigation, Johnson told the media, were those closest to Angela, her family and so-called friends. Johnson never provided details surrounding the cause of death, other than stating that it was "a clear-cut homicide." He referred all questions to Jenkins, who kept his mouth shut while Johnson tried to.

"The body was released to her family," said Johnson. "Strange, you think? We knew it was a criminal case because of her abrupt disappearance and four months later she was discovered in the river. The brothers lawyered up, and we found her car in the Western Drug parking lot. We searched it for clues, but there was no sign of blood or bullet holes or any other shit. Remember that her car was found the same day that the police report was filed—a couple days after she was last seen. Nobody at Western Drug recalled it being there in that spot the day before. No sign of Angela either until her body was found."

Police failed to impound the car she was driving at the time of her disappearance until her body was found. Months later, agents for the Montana Criminal Investigation Bureau took over the investigation into her death. Coverage of the case waned. Park County Attorney Tara DePuy was asked about the status of the investigation two years later, and she refused to reveal any details about her death and would not even reveal the cause of death. The silence was dictated by "the unusual nature of the case," she said. Tellingly, she said twice that the death was "not considered a suicide," and the investigation was a criminal one.

"For years, it was taboo or something to say that Angela's death was a murder investigation," said Johnson. "Who the hell knows why? She had been shot to death—execution style. It wasn't hard to determine that it was a homicide."

BROTHERS AS SUSPECTS

ANGELA'S TWIN BROTHERS, Kevin and Kelly Brown, were later named by Park County police officials as suspects in the death of their sister. According to published police reports, several witnesses told authorities that they recalled seeing Angela with her brothers shortly before she went missing, and that Angela had "a terrified look" on her face. Witnesses reasoned that the Brown brothers were still involved with the drug trade and still held criminal connections. In their backgrounds were narcotics distribution arrests. One police report noted that their father, Dale Brown, was known to be "a bully" and "violent" and had "often hurt his children."

One of the witnesses kept a copy of his police report and shared it. "I seen Angela with one of her brothers," recalled Livingston resident Paul Boehm in 2023. "I was driving my

'62 Impala convertible, and I was driving real slow. It was one of the twins she was with. She tried to signal me, I think. She was my neighbor out there, and she ran around with my daughter a lot. He had a pistol or something on him. It was on Ninth Street, and I didn't see whether they went on the island or not. Two weeks or a month later, it dawned on me when I seen her last, and I went down to the courthouse and told the detectives all the stories about it."

Kevin Lawrence Brown committed suicide in 2010, a shotgun in the mouth at age thirty-eight. His obituary described him as possessing "a magnanimous and exuberant personality" and said that he was predeceased by his sister Angela Brown and devoted rottweiler Zeus.

Angela Brown's murder remains unsolved. Within months of Angela's disappearance, her aunt, Sally Miller, the advocate who spearheaded the investigation, too, was dead, apparently the result of a "possible suicide," according to the coroner's report.

JEANNETTE ATWATER

MURDERED: JANUARY 16, 2000
MURDER LOCATION: BILLINGS

BORN IN MILES CITY and a graduate of Dawson County High School in Glendive, Jeannette Atwater was a mother of three, starting a new career and recuperating from donating a kidney to an ailing uncle.

Some called her by her nickname, "Charlie." Those who knew and loved her said that she was "gregarious" and "well-liked" and "outgoing."

"I don't ever recall seeing Charlie mad or discontent," said Charlotte Evers. "I knew her for fifteen years. She could cook, and she was handy—could replace her own car parts or screen doors or window screens or whatever. Sometimes we would sneak out at midnight to have a few cheeseburgers and talk and laugh. Her children were completely in love with her. She worked hard for them, and it was coming together for her."

Indeed, Atwater seemed to have turned a healthy corner in her life. She had started a new job, shifting away from a variety of bar and restaurant jobs to a position at the NAPA Auto Parts Distribution Center. The new position offered a future and stability and some benefits she hadn't experienced before. A few years earlier, she was putting in forty-five hours a week or more baking at a Billings restaurant for $5.75 an hour.

She made friends easily at her new job. And when she was invited to a holiday party and celebration with coworkers, she gladly accepted.

January 15, 2000. Atwater enjoyed an evening out with the NAPA crew. Then she met the wrong person.

"She was just a young lady trying to make a good living and a better life for herself and her kids," said one of the original investigating officers who worked the Atwater homicide.

OUT WITH FRIENDS; VEHICLE DISCOVERED IN FLAMES

ATWATER'S THREE YOUNG CHILDREN—the oldest of whom was a preteen—were in Washington with their father, from whom she was separated. She had a new job, a new sense of freedom, and a new outlook on life. After the NAPA company banquet in the afternoon, Atwater went alone to a bar where she used to work—the Eagle's Nest bar—and she stayed there for a short time, mostly visiting with former coworkers.

Later that evening Atwater met up with a group of NAPA coworkers at the Player's Club, a bar at 231 Main Street in the Heights. Atwater arrived alone, pulling up in her 1987 Cutlass Sierra.

At 8 p.m., she was at a table of five. The waitress brought them beer in half-gallon pitchers. The beer was cold, and the pitchers sweated and dripped. Her tiredness turned right away into lightheaded drunkenness.

She danced with at least one person there. But it seemed innocuous. She didn't talk with anyone for too long, didn't flirt, and didn't swap numbers. Atwater stayed at the bar until closing time, about 2 a.m.

After the bar closed, the group of NAPA folks congregated in the bar parking lot. They were celebrating the birthday of someone in the group in addition to belatedly marking the holidays. They exchanged presents and said their good-byes. But Atwater was already gone by then.

CAR FIRE REPORTED

Two HOURS LATER, at 3:32 a.m., a couple called 911 after seeing a car engulfed in spiraling flames. The car was burning in a gravel parking lot off Bench Boulevard near the city's bike path behind MetraPark. Firefighters had a hard time extinguishing the fire; all the doors were closed and locked, so they popped open the trunk. Inside, the firefighters found severely burned human remains, charred almost beyond recognition. The flames had blackened the person's features, and investigators at first were unsure if the body was male or female.

Dental records were used later that day to irrefutably identify Atwater. Investigators had already determined through the car registration, items of jewelry and clothing examined at autopsy, and information from her family that in all probability the victim was Atwater.

ASPHYXIATED IN TRUNK

According to her death certificate, Atwater's death was caused by asphyxiation or smoke inhalation, indicating that she was alive when she was placed in the trunk of her car.

Some aspects of the murder investigation, including whether Atwater was sexually assaulted or what toxicology reports revealed about her blood-alcohol level at the time of her death, have never been shared publicly.

Police have never commented on how they believe Atwater was placed in the trunk of her car. An autopsy showed no other obvious signs of fatal injury, such as bullet wounds or head trauma. She did not appear to have been gagged or bound.

The investigation showed that the fire was set intentionally, using an accelerant. Gasoline had been used to set the fire, and an empty gasoline container and a book of matches were found on the ground nearby. One set of vehicle tracks led into the gravel parking lot. A single set of footprints from the driver's door headed out to Bench Boulevard until they hit pavement.

TIME-STAMPED SURVEILLANCE MAY HAVE CAPTURED KILLER

DEPUTIES CANVASSED THE AREA for convenience stores open that night. Across Main Street from the Player's Club was a twenty-four-hour Cenex station. It had a number of surveillance cameras. One of the detectives decided to watch the footage from every one of its recording devices. Out of the grainy black and white footage, perhaps a monster would come into sight.

Shortly after 3 a.m., a car pulled in at the outermost pumps of the station. Out stepped a white or Native American male thought to be in his thirties; about five feet, ten inches tall; perhaps 180 pounds or so. Oily looking, acne scared, with brown, greasy hair, he was wearing blue pants and a blue warm-up jacket or jogging suit. His teeth were awful. His sideburns were unkempt and bristly. But his most prominent feature was noticeable pock marks on both cheeks. He was driving a mid-size brown, two-door hatchback car with an orange stripe.

Video surveillance, time-stamped at 3:09 a.m., shows the very same man inside the store standing at the counter. The clerk said the man bought a dollar's worth of gas, grabbed a pack of matches from the counter and left. Investigators noticed that the matches for customers at the store were similar to the matches found near Atwater's car.

The clerk said she didn't know whether the man put the gas into the car or a container or if he was alone. One witness said that he leaned against the rear end of the vehicle, shook an Old Gold or Marlboro out of his pack, and lit a cigarette.

"During the course of our investigation, we learned that a male subject had come into the Cenex store, across from the fire and across from the bar, and had purchased a dollar's worth of gas," said Yellowstone County Sheriff Mike Linder. "He put one dollar of gasoline into a gas can; and while he was in the store, he also grabbed a book of matches and he left with this, and that was about a half hour before the car had been found burning there."

Law enforcement followed up on a few calls about the person in question. Still, they had no identification. Detectives chased down numerous tips on the vehicle. No luck. They painstakingly eliminated all the vehicles around the Billings area and outlying places that matched that type.

"Whoever bought that stuff at the convenience store is still out there with that little car," Billings police detective Ron Wilson told the *Billings Gazette* in 2001. "Someone knows him. Even as bad as the photo is, if you know him, you can pick him out."

FEATURED ON *AMERICA'S MOST WANTED*

In the spring of 2000, the crime-fighting juggernaut *America's Most Wanted* ran a segment on the Atwater case that featured enhanced video of the greasy, seedy man seen at a nearby convenience store shortly before Atwater's burning car was found. Host John Walsh pleaded with audience members to circulate the image of the suspect as much as possible.

"The clerk who sold the man the gasoline was not able to provide a very detailed physical description," said Walsh, "but told the police that the suspect reeked of an overpowering stench of aftershave. Now that's not much to go on. But let's make sure to put this creep behind bars."

Years passed; the creepy boogeyman never emerged from the celluloid of the surveillance footage; the case stalled.

As far as forensics, ample evidence was collected from both Atwater's body and her car, such as hair and fibers, but the Montana Crime Lab was unable to ascertain enough information to connect the dots and close the loop. The case was made even more difficult because there was no substantial trace evidence, such as DNA or fingerprints.

Yellowstone County sheriff's department tapped into federal sources alerting them to similar crimes. But justice for this horrific murder has long been denied.

A LIFE OF "CHARLIE"

JEANNETTE ATWATER WAS BORN in Miles City January 14, 1966. Her nickname originated before she was born when her mother was at the Custer County Fair. Her mother's brother, Jim, won a stuffed donkey and gave it to his pregnant sister, saying "Here, this is for little Charlie!" Atwater's mother and father divorced when she was young. But she was exceptionally close to both parents. She even ended up with loving stepparents on both sides, both of whom later appeared on the *America's Most Wanted* broadcast and were reduced to sniffles and tears when talking about her.

Atwater graduated from Dawson County High School in Glendive in 1986 and attended Montana State University Billings (MSUB) on a volleyball scholarship. She proved to be especially effective as a middle blocker and setter and led the team in digs and kills her freshman year. A knee injury ended her athletic career, and she dropped out of college after just one quarter. Atwater left Montana and went to live near her father and stepmother in Bellingham, Washington. She enrolled in a technical college and took a number of automotive repair courses.

"I met her in an engine repair class," said Evers. "For a grease monkey, she had the clearest eyes, the straightest look, the most honest face—I miss it so."

In 1987 she joined the air force. She hoped to make a career in the military. But Atwater lasted only three months beyond basic training when she decided military life was not for her. She returned to Bellingham, where she met and married Robert Aiken, a chef and restaurateur, in 1990. The couple's children were born in 1990, 1992, and 1994.

They split in 1995. About two years after the divorce, Atwater moved back to Billings hoping to make another new start in a familiar and friendly place. Atwater was active in a local softball league, and she worked several waitress and bar jobs. Atwater dated but never found herself in another serious or long-term relationship.

THEORIES OF MURDER NIXED

NOT LONG BEFORE HER DEATH she had been to Washington, where she donated a kidney to an uncle. In November 1999, the surgery was done at a Seattle hospital. "Charlie" didn't think twice about making such a sacrifice. The kids stayed with their father in Washington while Atwater returned to Montana and recuperated from the kidney donation.

She was divorced, but Atwater and her ex-husband parted amiably. He had no ties to Billings or Montana—in fact, he was happily living a productive life elsewhere. Detectives questioned him extensively, and he was quickly eliminated from suspicion.

Atwater had danced with a man she met at the Player's Club, but the man left alone before closing time. The man was identified and questioned by detectives. He met Atwater at the bar, he said, and they danced together a few times before going their separate ways. He, too, was eliminated from the suspect pool.

Not long before her death, she had started a new position at the NAPA Auto Parts Distribution Center. None of her coworkers were ever seriously considered to be connected to the crime. Atwater had no gambling or drug addictions or financial trouble that could help detectives establish a possible motive for her murder.

The hardest part to swallow for Ron Wilson of the Yellowstone County Sheriff's Office was that he could never pinpoint how Atwater exited the bar. He was sure that she did not leave with the group of NAPA coworkers, and he could never determine whether she went out the front door or the back door or how she even left the bar.

People who were in the bar parking lot after closing said they did not recall seeing Atwater or her car. Bar employees monitoring the parking lot couldn't recall anything suspicious. Equally problematic for investigators, not a single person recalled seeing any type of disturbance or problem; no altercation had drawn anybody's attention; no struggle; no strange people loitering or groveling or intimidating. By about 2:15 a.m., the parking lot was virtually empty, except the approximately six vehicles of the bar staff.

"SENSELESS" MURDER WITHOUT RESOLUTION

MOST PEOPLE WHO HAVE WORKED the Atwater case seem to believe her death was a random act of violence by some depraved cretin passing through, and she just happened to be in the wrong place at the wrong moment. If that is the case, it could have been anyone that fatal night. Desperate to find some evidence, investigators who reopened the case a few years ago even considered a monster truck show in Billings the weekend of Atwater's death, and police did their best to try to make contact with the event's out-of-area spectators and participants.

Detective Ron Wilson said that he has been haunted ever after by the vicious murder of Atwater and by how someone could be so numb and indifferent to taking a life.

"This one just seems more senseless than others," Wilson told the Associated Press in 2009. "We can't find a reason for it. We don't know how he got her. It's a mystery. It might have been a random act. Maybe it was someone with the opportunity. Maybe it was someone in the community that decided this was something they were going to do. It's very, very hard to say."

Atwater was buried in Forsyth.

DARLENE WILCOCK

MURDERED: APRIL 17, 2003
MURDER LOCATION: KALISPELL

SHORTLY AFTER MIDNIGHT April 17, 2003. The lightning was flashing, and the rain fell in sheets. Kalispell police responded to a call at Motel 6 in south Kalispell. Officers found the body of twenty-six-year-old Darlene Wilcock lying on a bed, with signs of brutality and strangulation. Manifold abrasions covered the skull, and blood leaked onto the sheets from the base of the skull. Her fingertips were bloody, and her arms dangled limply off the bed. A trickle of blood flowed from the corner of her mouth.

The crime scene examination immediately proved to be uniquely complicated: Multiple men's DNA samples were found in the area and on her body; a fiancé had a resounding motive in the insurance policy; sexual activity was indicated with a man Wilcock by all accounts loathed; physical evidence belonged to a wicked, sadistic Kalispell businessman who was leading an archetypal double life.

Investigators knew that they had a complex mystery to solve in the Motel 6 slaying and the secrecy of the interior world of Darlene Wilcock.

SOCIAL AUTOPSY OF DARLENE WILCOCK

DARLENE JEAN WILCOCK was born in Spokane, Washington, on January 5, 1977, the oldest of five siblings. Family

Shortly after midnigh, April 17, 2003. The lightning was flashing and the rain fell in sheets. Kalispell police responded to a call at the Motel 6 in south Kalispell. Officers found the body of 26-year-old Darlene Wilcock lying on a bed, with signs of brutality and strangulation. Police named three different men as possible perpetrators in the homicide. No arrests have ever been made in the case.
COURTESY AUTHOR'S COLLECTION

members describe her as "caring" and "loving," with an innate gift for helping people when they most needed it. She loved the outdoors and traveling. In some ways, she had no choice. A military child, upheaval was one constant in Darlene's life, the family addresses crisscrossing from the Deep South to the West Coast and the Rocky Mountain states in between. Shyly introverted, Darlene graduated from high school in Southern California.

"She was the typical nineties product in high school," said her sister Holly Blouch. "She loved heavy metal, and she always wore black. She loved Metallica and Nirvana. She always wore stonewash jeans."

Though she had a mostly lighthearted disposition, Darlene's upbringing was marked by heartache: her father was emotionally and physically abusive, and her mother was timid and frightened of him and his exhibitions of violence. He had a crew cut and an authoritative manner. And he had a sadistic streak. According to available records, Ernest Wilcock left the military and found work as a police officer in Montana, and he was terminated and sent to prison after he was accused and found guilty of soliciting sex from women at traffic stops and shooting into the vehicle of one woman who tried to escape his perverted ensnarement. The state of Montana sentenced Wilcock to six hundred months in Montana State Prison in 1997 for sexual intercourse without consent.

After Ernest was sent to prison, Darlene was the surrogate parent to her younger siblings, and she missed a lot of days in junior high school and high school taking care of them.

"She had a rough, rough childhood," said Blouch. "Our grandmothers on both sides, they didn't seem to like her a lot; they were stern and strict with her. We moved a lot, and it was rougher on Darlene than the rest of us. She was the oldest, and our dad (Ernest) was in prison. Our mom was working two jobs, and Darlene had to also be the mom, cooking, helping with homework, and doing all of the parental responsibilities."

"We didn't have an easy childhood," said Brandi Bauer, Darlene's sister. "Our father was never a father to us. He'd been in and out of prison, for trading sex and sexual misconduct. He went to jail for endangering the public. Darlene had it rougher than most. Mom had to work two, three jobs to support us. Responsibilities landed on Darlene's shoulders. She needed to get the younger kids up for school and to do homework. She had the responsibilities of the parent without being the parent."

Darlene arrived in Kalispell, Montana, after high school. She liked to collect agates and geodes and found comfort in the LDS church and found employment at Wendy's. She embraced all the cultural icons of country living, from the music of Garth Brooks and Reba McIntire to the sort of attire that you'd expect to see in that genre.

Darlene loved to play billiards in the local bars and listen to country and western music in the jukebox, often bedecked in blue jeans and cowboy boots and festooned with a shiny belt buckle with a large "J," the first letter of her middle name.

At Wendy's she was promoted to shift manager and enjoyed it. There she fell in love with one of her coworkers, Randy Jones. Darlene and Randy both worked to become shift managers. They moved in together following a couple of months of dating.

Both Darlene and Randy visualized something larger than Kalispell, something more financially hopeful than Wendy's. The couple decided to attend trucking school. Commanding big rigs would allow for a greater income and provide the couple with an opportunity to explore cities and states, a plethora of places previously unseen. They received their over-the-road trucking CDL certification on the same day in the spring of 2002, and both were hired soon thereafter at Watkins-Glenn.

"She was a lean, scrawny girl, and it was some sight watching her tie down those big loads," said Blouch. "Trucking was good for Darlene. She was proud of her accomplishments. She had a lot of self-esteem from it."

But she tired of the untethered trucking lifestyle and returned to the security of Kalispell. She missed her family and the expansive waters of Flathead Lake and the largely tranquil spirit of small-town western Montana living. She landed a job at Stream, a technology company, as a receptionist. Holly worked there, too, in the accounts receivable department. And she had started a new routine—work, drinking with coworkers, bowling with some of the same ones, darts, billiards, and brassy jokes at the bar.

"Why she came home from being on the road nobody really knows," said Blouch. "She loved the job at Stream and being back home. She liked going out and dancing at the Blue Moon and enjoying the music there. Life was better. It seemed."

Still, there was something secretive about Darlene. One time Holly found Darlene sitting in her car in the parking lot at Stream. She was plopped in the passenger's seat, staring out the window, a queer countenance on her face: a little reserved, a little melancholy, a little proud. Even her closest sibling had a hard time reading her expression.

Randy Jones followed Darlene to Montana. But he didn't return to Kalispell, instead shifting his base to Missoula. He continued to work as a long-haul truck driver. There were signs that Randy wasn't treating Darlene correctly on the road, and she told her sisters that she was grateful to be in a safe place away from the instability of his explosiveness. She later told one friend that Randy had slapped her with such sudden violence she had caromed off the center table and went sprawling on her hands and knees. With her sisters, she was less forthcoming.

"The last time that Darlene came home from the road to visit she had a badly split lip," said Brandi Bauer. "Her upper lip was split, and she had a purple bruise on her neck, down to her chest. She said that she had fallen off the bed and hit the dresser, but her whole neck and chest had been bruised."

One year later, she was slain.

MURDER WASN'T RANDOM

FROM THE OUTSET of the investigation, authorities were unwilling to release too many details. But Kalispell Police Chief Frank Garner did reveal that law enforcement "strongly believed" that Darlene knew her killer, that her murder "wasn't random," and that the clues to solving her death could be found in the examination of her relationships. Perhaps she had had multiple relations in the hotel room that night? Garner said that Darlene had quaffed several glasses of champagne on the night of the murder, but the champagne bottle placed in the bathroom sink had been wiped of fingerprints. Only one champagne glass was found.

SUSPECT №1: MATT DAY

POLICE IMMEDIATELY IDENTIFIED Matthew Day as a suspect in the murder of Wilcock. According to police reports and news accounts and recorded interviews, Matt is the last known person to see Darlene alive. In his deposition, he talks about Darlene intimately, and mentions on more than one occasion that he and she were "a thing" and "in a relationship" and that they were going "to have a life."

"We can tell you that Mr. Day is an ex-roommate of Wilcock's, and he is one of the foremost persons of interest," said John Stock, Kalispell police detective. "I can tell you that he has, by and large, wholly refused to cooperate, and that's put us in a difficult position. He is at the top of the list."

"Matt used to be friends with my husband," said Blouch. "Matt Day and Darlene had a mutual friend, and at one point they all lived together and moved into my mom's house. He kept trying to get Darlene to go out with him. We kept him

away from her because she couldn't stand him and kept trying
to avoid him and wanted us to keep him away from her. He
kept pressuring her to go out with him.

"We felt bad for him, and we moved him into our home,"
she continued. "Our mother felt badly for him and wanted to
be nice. He never held a job. He has always lived off of people
or used people. He hasn't talked to our family since the day it
happened. Darlene never liked Matt. His DNA was on her,
and him being seen with her the last day she was alive? She
absolutely, positively despised this man. Every chance she got,
she would run away from him. She never wanted to be alone
with him. She'd run into the other room."

"All of the information we've gathered tells us that Darlene
didn't want to be in any type of relationship with him," said
Detective Stock. "But Mr. Day's DNA is located in the motel
room that night? The last place that she was seen alive was the
Finish Line Cocktail Lounge and Casino. Mr. Day was seen
with her at that time."

According to police, Day spoke freely and without counsel
two times for a total of approximately six hours. The third
time police asked him to come to the station, he lawyered up.

According to Matt Day's interview with police detectives,
after he was told that Darlene was found dead, he told investigators that he "just saw her the night before at the Finish
Lane at about 7 p.m.," and she was going to meet up again
with him that night "around midnight" after she went to the
motel to 'beautify herself.' "

"That's not how my sister talked," said Blouch. "Darlene
doesn't talk like that. She is a truck driver. She might have said,
I will get cleaned up, or give me some time to get changed.
I know that she never would have told anyone that she was
going to 'beautify herself'. Anyone that knew Darlene knew

that she couldn't stand Matt and didn't want to be around him. Those two stories don't add up."

SUSPECT №2: RANDY JONES

Police identified Randy Jones as another suspect in the murder of Darlene Wilcock.

"Randy was always showing everyone affection, except Darlene," said Holly. "Before she met Randy, we were super close. We had her going to the Mormon Church and active and doing activities. The more involved she became with him, the more she moved away from the church. By the end of Darlene's life, she became very secretive. We don't know if she planned to meet someone at the hotel. She wouldn't discuss who or where or why. That wasn't the type of person that she was."

"Randy knew how to turn on the charm," said Bauer. "He always knew what to say and when to say it and how to make someone believe it. Darlene dated when she was in California, but Randy was probably her second most serious and solid relationship. She gave up a lot for him. Randy was flirtatious with our younger sister, buying her inappropriate clothes. He was flirtatious with me and everybody."

According to Darlene's mother, Marla Friske, Randy had Darlene under an old spell of sorts.

"Too quickly," said Friske. "Dating to living together. Giving up their jobs and apartment. Going out on the road and becoming truck drivers. It was supposed to be equal. But Randy set it up that he was an owner-operator, and she worked for him. He promised to marry her. She thought that she was his fiancée. Why else would she open those accounts and make him the top dog?"

Darlene died without having made a will, and Marla was named the personal representative of the estate. At the time of her death, she possessed two substantial insurance policies, each worth $250,000, each opened in December 2002. The main beneficiary of these policies was Randy Jones. Holly was the alternate recipient of the State Farm Life Insurance Company policy, and Brandi was the alternate recipient of the Farmers New World Life Insurance Company policy.

After Darlene's death, sisters Holly Blouch and Brandi Bauer brought numerous actions against Randy, seeking a share of the insurance proceeds and brought a wrongful death and survivorship claim against Randy. In the lawsuit, Darlene's sisters contend that Randy was the person who Darlene was planning to meet at the Kalispell Motel 6 on April 17, 2003.

"She lived in town, but the motel room was sort of her getaway," said Bauer. "It served the purpose for Darlene, and that's where she would meet her Randy. He was still working as a long-haul truck driver, and he would come to Kalispell."

According to retired Kalispell Police Chief Roger Nasset, Wilcock's former fiancé made sense as a suspect for a few reasons: money, money, money.

"We think that Mr. Jones convinced Darlene to place him as the primary beneficiary of her life insurance plan shortly before her death," Nasset said in 2023. "There was a major legal battle over the money. In our investigation we learned that Mr. Jones was already married, in Missoula I believe, when he was with Darlene, and that's something that greatly diminished his credibility in police statements. We know that Mr. Jones arrived in town unexpectedly right before Wilcock was murdered. His DNA was at the Motel 6 that night."

SUSPECT №3: KALISPELL BUSINESSMAN DICK DASEN

ANOTHER PERSON OF INTEREST in the case from the onset was Dick Dasen Sr., a Kalispell businessman who was later sentenced to prison for operating a meth-for-sex prostitution ring. Investigators have never laid out the case against Dasen, except noting that his DNA was found in the hotel room and that he and a small-town politician from Missouri named Casey Guernsey were swept up in an illicit drug-sex-money laundering sting, and both men were tied to Wilcock.

"We don't believe that Darlene was involved in prostitution, per se," said a Kalispell investigator close to the case. "When you look at all of the players, nothing surprises us when it comes to this case."

In May 2023, a judge denied Dasen's latest request for probation release.

LUCKY TO BE REMEMBERED, SAYS SISTER

NO ONE HAS BEEN CRIMINALLY CHARGED in connection with Wilcock's death. Matt Day did not return multiple requests to be interviewed. Randy Jones could not be located. Dick Dasen, according to Kalispell authorities, is still considered a suspect in the murder of Wilcox.

"We feel lucky when people still remember Darlene," said Holly. "The attitude is that victims like Darlene just don't mean anything to anyone but some family members. That they are not important. Darlene lived in a small town, and she was not rich, and she was not well known or popular. Because of that, it seems like nobody cares enough to get it out there."

Matt Day refused multiple requests to speak in person, but he did agree to answer questions via email. His responses to more than fifty questions were all answered either yes or no. He maintains that he and Darlene were in a consensual relationship and denies having anything to do with Darlene's murder. Randy Jones did not respond to multiple interview requests.

BARBARA BOLICK

VANISHED: JULY 18, 2007
VANISHED FROM: CORVALLIS

Whenever we go hiking, we take for granted that we will return to our vehicle, whether solo or with our hiking partners. Barbara Bolick surely expected the same thing in Corvallis, Montana, on July 18, 2007.

She was supposed to have been gone only a few hours that morning, out on a two-mile roundtrip hike with a friend; they were destined for the Bear Creek Overlook in the Bitterroot Mountains. An experienced hiker and very familiar with the area, Bolick would not have considered the Bear Creek Overlook to be much of a chore. The overlook trail was a short, well-trodden path, a popular destination because of its gigantic payoff of scenery and short investment of exertion to get there. Indeed, the staggering view was what brought Barbara back time after time—and for one final time.

Sometime between 11:30 a.m. and 1 p.m., Barbara and a male friend lounged, snacked, and relaxed at the scenic overlook. She ventured to the edge, approximately twenty to thirty feet from him. He looked north and then he looked east. When he turned around about a minute later—she was gone. At least that's the story he has told investigators ever since. And they were never able to prove or disprove the man's account.

TWO MALE WITNESSES SOUGHT

ON THE MORNING OF Barbara's disappearance, the road leading up the Bear Creek Overlook trailhead was blocked less
than a mile down the hill; a Forest Service crew worked to
replace a damaged culvert.

By the time the crew arrived at approximately 11 a.m., a
pair of vehicles already were parked at the road closure sign:
one driven by Barbara and her friend, sporting number 13
Bitterroot Valley tags; and a fair-colored, older model Chevrolet S-10 SUV with Missoula County license plates.

The Forest Service crew was patching the drain when a pair
of young men in their early twenties came strolling into their
work site: clean-cut, well-tanned, average builds, physically fit.
One of them had a considerably darker complexion than the
other. One was described as "dark-skinned with black hair,"
and the other had "a medium complexion and reddish hair."

The group remembered the small black collie with droopy
ears and white spots that jumped in the chilly runoff. The men
stopped and talked for a bit and then walked off, seemingly
without a worry. Nothing about the men's behavior indicated
that they were concerned or bothered by anything other than
savoring the summer heat.

According to the first Ravalli County Sheriff's Department
press release, neither of the men was considered a suspect in
any wrongdoing, but officials believed that they could provide
valuable information.

The attendant at the gas station three miles from the trailhead remembered seeing a pair of men matching the police
description. The dark youth had pumped gas and had come
into the glass-fronted office only to pay. The attendant said
that the other young man opened the truck of their car and

rifled through and rearranged the contents. He said the car had several bumper stickers, but he couldn't recall what exactly they'd said. The man at the back of the car had a hunting knife attached to his hip.

FRIEND OF VICTIM SUSPECTED

AN EXTENSIVE SEARCH OF THE AREA turned up no trace of Bolick. Below the overlook Ravalli County Search and Rescue found a number of unusual items, but they could not say for certain if they were connected to her disappearance: two filthy $1 bills, some loose change, a skeleton key on a rusty key ring, a dried rabbit's foot, a putty knife, and a scrap of dirty yellow notebook paper folded into a small square.

The friend who accompanied her on the hike "cooperated with investigators and talked his head off," said Ravalli County Sheriff Dale Dye, who said that he didn't believe that Bolick "left this earth of her own free will."

According to Dye, Bolick was an active and present mother to her two children, who were staying with relatives in Oregon that week. "She loved them dearly, as far as we know." None of Bolick's belongings had been missing, including her pet dog and cat, jewelry, billfold, driver's license, and passport. The golden retriever–Labrador mix she had adopted ten years before at the humane society. Her cat was almost twenty years old. All her childhood keepsakes were still at the house.

Carl Bolick contacted several media outlets and told one TV affiliate that evening that his wife "was afraid of heights" and would not have gone near the edge of a steep cliff or left the trail without force. "She was an experienced hiker, and this wasn't the type of hike that you'd even bring a water bottle," he said.

Various police documents described Carl as "a cooperative and forthcoming witness," and one officer quickly declared that he was "never seriously considered to have had anything to do" with Barbara's disappearance.

MORNING OF BARBARA'S DISAPPEARANCE

BARBARA MET CARL when he was an air force officer working on an air base in New Jersey. They decided later to move to Montana, but Barbara disliked the endless, open winds and overall void of activity of his hometown in Dillon. One summer Barbara fell in love with the Bitterroots, and the couple eventually bought land near Darby. Afterward they purchased a home near Corvallis. Barbara joined several hiking clubs and found a part-time job at an outdoor-adventure store. Carl liked to hike, too, and they used to hike and camp frequently together. Then Carl had a minor heart attack while on the trail to Bass Lake, and he decided that he couldn't go hiking any longer. Still, Barbara hiked every canyon and summit in the area, and she came to understand the Bitterroot Mountains quite well.

In July 2007, Carl and Barbara had been married for fourteen years, and she was always keen to show and share the scenery from Bear Creek Overlook with visitors that her husband would invite. On the morning of July 18, Barbara volunteered to take Jim Ramaker, fifty-eight, a friend of her husband's cousin, Marguerite, both from California, to the overlook. Ramaker, a semiretired woodworker, and Marguerite, a seamstress, had driven from the San Diego area together and had just begun dating. The couple arrived a few days earlier and stayed with the Bolicks.

By 8 a.m. the sun had just burned through the morning mist, and its rays came slanting down through the trees. Red Fox Lane was streaked with sunbeams. It would be the perfect conditions for a beautiful morning hike.

According to Carl's police statement, Carl's cousin was feeling the effects of one too many frozen margaritas the night before at a Mexican restaurant in Victor and decided not to go that morning. Carl was still sleeping when Barbara came and told him she and Ramaker were going hiking to the overlook. The last thing he told her was not to worry about dinner. "I will take care of cooking dinner," he said.

Barbara and Jim walked out the door sometime between 8:30 and 9 a.m. Carl followed them to the car. Barbara had a blue windbreaker to go with her blue sneakers. Her features were lean and chiseled, perhaps from many straight weeks of strenuous hikes and swimming in cold lakes. She commented to Carl that she was amazed that they had pretty, spring flowers still in their yard. She had many flower beds, with beautiful flowers growing in them.

Carl spent the morning drinking coffee and working on a small carpentry project. He tinkered with a model car and read a book about local geology. When noon rolled around, his cousin started getting a little uneasy about the fact that Barbara and Jim hadn't returned. Ramaker was "a trusted family acquaintance," according to Carl, so he wasn't overly concerned.

At fifty-five, Barbara was an avid hiker who at five feet tall and about 115 pounds kept herself trim and healthy by running, riding, and taking long walks into the mountains. And as an added touch of safety, Carl knew she had the .357 Magnum pistol he'd bought her stowed away in her daypack. Once he stopped coming along on hikes, he figured that a pistol would be a peace-of-mind replacement. He'd always tell her to not pack the weapon too deeply in the backpack; if she suddenly met up with a mountain lion or a bear, she would not have time to dig around to find it.

According to Carl's police statement, by 1:30 p.m., Marguerite was getting antsy. He told her to calm down. Barbara was an experienced hiker, and this hike didn't require much fortitude or skill. He suggested that perhaps they'd had a flat tire—it was a twenty-mile drive to the Bear Creek Overlook trailhead from their home—or stopped somewhere to have a hamburger and a beer. An hour passed. Carl agreed with Marguerite; he needed to call somebody. About that time, the phone rang. It was a Forest Service law enforcement officer who immediately asked Carl if his wife's name was Barbara.

Barbara had been reported missing—by Jim Ramaker. Carl told the officer he'd meet her at the trailhead.

Forest Service officials had Ramaker detained for questioning. The two male hikers were spotted at about 11:30 a.m., and Ramaker walked into the very same Forest Service maintenance site at about 1 p.m. and asked the trail crew if they'd seen Barbara. One of the road crew walked with him back to Barbara's vehicle, and there was no trace of her. Ramaker marched back up to the overlook one more time.

When he returned approximately an hour and a half later, he told the crew he needed assistance. He said he couldn't find Barbara anywhere.

Ramaker told investigators later that he and Barbara stopped at the overlook and had a granola bar, some crackers, and a bottle of water. He told them that they'd seen the two young men and said something like, "It's a beautiful day, isn't it?"

Ramaker told Forest Service officials and police that the pair sat and snacked and enjoyed the mountain views for approximately thirty or forty minutes. Ramaker said Barbara was only about twenty or thirty feet away when he turned to take one more look at the scenery. He said that he looked toward St. Mary's Peak and commented on the crystal clearness of the sky.

It was a fleeing head tilt, possibly forty-five seconds, possibly a minute. According to Ramaker, when he turned around, Barbara was gone. It was the last time he saw her, he told investigators.

INVESTIGATORS SKEPTICAL OF HER FRIEND'S STORY

"It was really a tough one for me to understand and believe this whole crazy thing from the start," Perry Johnson, the lead investigator on the case for the Ravalli County Sheriff's Department, said in 2023. "I haven't been able to find anyone else who's had a similar experience. We're talking about a minute, and then you look back and she's gone. How could that possibly happen?"

From the start Johnson said he believed the key to the case stood in identifying the two young men hiking the trail that day. He assumed they were local guys because of the Missoula license plates and the fact that they were hiking on a Wednesday morning.

Johnson was clear in his belief that he did not suspect them of doing anything wrong; he wanted the men to confirm that Bolick was there that morning. They weren't in hot water.

"I never had a witness to confirm or conflict with the information that we'd gathered, and these guys were the key to solving the whole thing," he said.

REWARD AND SEARCH FRUITLESS

THE FAMILY OF BARBARA BOLICK—Barbara and Carl had two children, a son and a daughter—offered a $10,000 reward for information leading to the two men's identification. Johnson told a Missoula television station, half joking, that the two men could even collect the reward themselves.

Right after her disappearance, the sheriff's department deployed search teams, brought in highly trained dogs, and even called in high-tech infrared helicopters to scour the area. Unfortunately, they never found a single incriminating thing.

Days later, Ramaker and Carl's cousin, Marguerite, returned to San Diego, and he was said to have continued to cooperate in the investigation. Until something else happened—the discovery of Barbara's body or the glaring indicators of foul play—he would remain solely a witness. Indeed, Johnson said that he wanted to be open minded.

"There is no good evidence that Ramaker or anyone else did anything to Barbara," said Johnson in a Ravalli County Sheriff's memo to the press.

In a newspaper interview six months after the disappearance, Carl said that the hardest part to fathom was that Barbara disappeared on the trail that was so easy to hike. He rattled off a litany of theories and rumors that had been circulating in the Bitterroot Valley. A number of people thought foul play was involved. Others wondered if "a wildly strange mountain man" spotted in the area might have played a part. Most of them Carl likely dismissed as absurd. Still others asked Carl if he thought perhaps his wife had simply walked away, moved on, or had escaped. One of the odder aspects of the situation was that, as time passed, fewer and fewer people wanted to talk about Barbara.

"It's to the point that people don't want to bring it up anymore," Carl told the *Bitterroot Star*. "It's too emotional. . . . The only answer that I have right now is that I just don't know. I don't know what happened to her."

With no suspects and a whole bunch of extensive interviews with Ramaker, the case never moved forward.

"I doubt someone would be able to grab her without Ramaker being aware that some altercation was going on," Johnson said. "We can't eliminate foul play; nor can we suggest foul play. We just don't know."

Barbara's daughter, who requested that her last name be withheld to maintain her privacy, echoed the detective's words. "I've gone over and over and over this again and again, and I don't have any answers," she said. "It doesn't add up. No answers. No theories. It doesn't make any sense."

After nineteen missions scouring nearly all the trails and surrounding areas on both sides of the Bitterroot Valley, and thousands of hours spent by Ravalli County and Missoula County Search and Rescue teams, volunteers, law enforcement, Lifeflight, Careflight, Montana Air Guard, and Forest Service, the search was called off.

BARBARA'S FRIEND'S ACCOUNT QUESTIONED

SOON, PERRY JOHNSON WAVERED on his treatment of Ramaker as a suspect. On one hand, he said that he wanted to "be fair" and treat him as "a witness." On the other hand, he repeatedly made comments and statements that undermined the impression of neutrality and evenhandedness.

"I don't think she was or is up there," Johnson told KPAX in the summer of 2008. "I mean, no one else that has been interviewed saw Barbara up there."

Perhaps feeling a sense of helplessness, Johnson publicly expressed his suspicion of Ramaker and even today still goes so far as to question the truthfulness of his version of events.

"Ramaker is the only source that Barbara Bolick was up there that day," said Johnson in 2023. "I've always wondered if Barbara was ever up at the Overlook in the first place. We will never know now."

For the remainder of his life, Carl would gaze across the kitchen table and the Bitterroot Valley to the area where his wife vanished off the face of the Earth. He eventually remarried in 2013 and died in November 2021. Jim Ramaker, age seventy-four, lives in California. He denied multiple requests to be interviewed.

JAMEE CHRISTINE GROSSMAN

VANISHED: MARCH 16, 2012
VANISHED FROM: LOCKWOOD

FRIDAY, MARCH 16, 2012. Lockwood, Montana. Jamee Christine Grossman, twenty-five, was one of about twenty mostly young adults at a birthday party. She was there with her boyfriend, Frank Hammontree. The party kicked into overdrive at around midnight, and enough alcohol was stocked to keep the last of the revelers buzzed until about 4 a.m. The last keg was drained right about then.

When the other guests woke up, the blue-eyed, strawberry-blonde-haired woman "with the most brilliant and trusting smile," as one friend described it, was gone.

Hammontree told police on March 20, 2012, that at some point during the night, he and Jamee had an argument about a missing pot pipe and their rapidly increasing debts and that she had decided to leave on foot. He said he didn't try to stop her. He said he knew that it was bitterly cold and that she'd be vulnerable to foul weather and perhaps even worse, foul play, but that he didn't care. She said she was leaving. He cussed at her and nodded in the direction of the door.

Grossman, five feet, six inches and 130 pounds, graduated in 2005 from Billings Senior High School, and she still lived in Billings. She had two daughters. She had some minor skirmishes with the law and had some personal struggles, including anger management issues and court-ordered classes stemming from a traffic altercation that threw her into a blinding fury.

And on top of this, Jamee lived without solid ground underfoot. One week earlier, Grossman and Hammontree were living in a motel on 1st Avenue North. But the couple's difficulties with drugs and alcohol led to them being evicted. There was too much fighting, too many shady characters coming and going at all hours of the day. On Friday, March 16, the couple accepted an offer from friends to move into a trailer home on Hillner Lane in Lockwood, and then came the party.

Authorities didn't officially classify her as a missing person until late May as they were not especially certain that she hadn't been working in some illicit trade—selling drugs, prostitution—on Hammontree's behalf. Police and witness reports describe Hammontree as a "tall man with pockmarked skin" with hair "a dirty shade of black" and an old razor scar that cut a purple ridge from the lobe of his ear to the tip of his chin.

"He's from Chicago but lived with his grandparents at some point and went to high school there," said Billings detective Raymond Himes. "Don't know much else except for we are pretty sure he was an informant and was into prostitution and sex slavery. He has an extensive arrest record. He said Jamee walked away. Doesn't sound right, does it? But nobody at the party ever stepped forward to contradict him. Then he changed his song entirely and said that she was alive on Saturday. No one at the party would talk."

SUSPECT'S TWO CONFLICTING STATEMENTS

HAMMONTREE'S FIRST POLICE STATEMENT read like this: Grossman spent the night at the birthday party, and when he woke up the next morning, she was gone. Grossman left sometime between 1 and 2:30 a.m.

In his second police statement, weeks later, on May 29, 2012, however, he told investigators that on the morning of Saturday, March 17, 2012, he and Jamee had planned to move into the friend's trailer and that she had scheduled a meeting with the father of her children to have a visitation with them and called him at about 8:45 in the morning. Their father was the primary custodian, though he did allow for flexible visitations, with strict stipulations.

Hammontree said that he had taken Jamee to a convenience store on 1st Avenue North where that meeting was supposed to have taken place. He said that Jamee, feeling sick, wanted to cancel the meeting. But he convinced her to proceed. He said he saw Jamee get into a navy or cobalt-colored vehicle—an older model Pontiac Firebird Trans Am—and that was the last he saw of her.

But, according to public police reports, an examination of that convenience store's security cameras showed no Jamee, no Hammontree, no greeting father, no little girls, no flashy blue vehicle.

The third time police brought Hammontree down to the station, he had an attorney with him, the suspect clammed up, and the police didn't have enough to charge him with a murder rap. Hammontree strolled out of the station, smirking.

All other leads and tips that have come in have been exhausted.

JAMEE GROSSMAN: HAD THE WORLD BY THE TAIL

THE MOTHER OF TWO worked at Fiddler's Green sports bar and was employed at the Golden Corral on the west side of Billings. She had endured her fair share of hardships—broken relationships, drugs, low self-esteem. Her mother, Leslie Taft, said that her daughter was doing well in life and had enrolled in college, but then became distant about two years before the disappearance, soon after Jamee began dating Hammontree.

"He didn't like her being around anyone else or her family," said Taft. "He was controlling and manipulative, and he was devious."

Taft still wonders what her daughter's life would have been like had she not met Hammontree, what she'd look like in middle age, what she'd be doing for work.

"She had the world by the tail," said Taft. "She was a great mom, a great person. She was a loving girl. Then she quit school and slowly but surely faded into the background."

Taft last saw her daughter in early March, a few days before the party where Grossman was last seen. She conducted her own investigation and tried to extract as much information as she could from the other guests at the party. One of the attendees slammed the door in her face; another said she wished her luck, but she would not be able to talk about Jamee. She kept in regular communication with the detectives in charge of the case over the years, but she never heard any solid leads from any of them about where her daughter might be.

When she tried to call her daughter's cell phone, the number came back as disconnected. She scoured all the local bars and haunts that her daughter frequented. At her own risk, she followed the suspect and some of the suspect's friends, to their houses, to parties, to seemingly illicit transactions. One time she followed Hammontree to his mother's house, a tiny shack on the east rim of Billings, and he was with another girl, a blonde, close to Jamee's age, uncomfortably similar to her in looks.

Loud talk rang on the street corner. She sat and watched from an old railroad track with dogs barking on it. The pavement was all torn up. She sat in the car for about thirty minutes, empty and hurt and confused. Hatred of him was in her. It wasn't dominant. Fear was dominant. But hatred was there.

"I thought about confronting him, and I thought about doing far worse," said Taft. "I felt sick and nervous and strangely aggressive. I backed down the road."

Taft said she learned from police that somebody in the area had been using her daughter's identification, including at a pawn shop and a liquor mart, but that they "believe it wasn't Grossman," she said. Unfortunately, police were never able to apprehend the guilty party. The pawn shop didn't have surveillance cameras, and the lead was lost in a maze.

Taft said she was especially troubled when Hammontree, within weeks of the last sighting of Jamee, reported to several different people that "somebody had confronted him," according to both Taft and published records, and Hammontree told them Grossman "was dead and buried." At about the same time, a male in his mid-twenties said the same thing to Grossman's brother. The man cornered her brother in the grocery store and told him that she had been killed by a drug gang. He was drunk and didn't enunciate very clearly. He looked half contemptuous and half sorrowful.

"Hammontree came to my house and said he'd been confronted about Jamee," said Taft. "The same thing happened with her brother, saying they'd heard that she was dead. That's when we called the cops once again. That was toward the end of May. . . . It reeked like shit of a conspiracy. It seemed like it was something that was prearranged and planned to divert attention away from Hammontree. Two months after she was gone, police lifted themselves off of their asses and designated it a missing case."

Initial leads turned bitter—and stayed that way. The case has gone from complicated to impenetrable. A spokesperson from the Billings sheriff's department said that detectives are still actively investigating Grossman's disappearance but acknowledged that "without a body it makes it unlikely that anyone will ever be brought to prosecution and trial for murder."

As for Frank Hammontree, police still consider him the prime suspect in the disappearance and presumed murder of Grossman. He is currently serving a lengthy prison sentence for narcotics distribution and weapons and probation violations. He was sentenced in U.S. District Court in Billings in 2020 for brandishing a Hi-Point pistol and carrying two loaded magazines when the police arrested him for parole violations.

Many years ago, police named Ryan Anthony Cislo, a hard-edged drug trafficker, as a possible accomplice in the case. Cislo committed suicide in June 2022.

As for Taft, she has heard all the same statements and lines before. She has heard the same responses about how no new leads exist, tips have dried up, witnesses have clammed up, how hunches aren't enough to make arrests, how probabilities do not make facts. She lived all the general stages of grief: denial, anger, depression, and acceptance. She said that she longs for the day to feel something unfamiliar: relief.

"People know what happened to Jamee," said Taft. "I truly hope that someday all of those people with information— friends, friends of her boyfriend, all of the possible witnesses, anyone else—come forward to help aid and assist police with the investigation."

For many years Taft put up posters and handed out fliers soliciting information that could potentially place Jamee's killer in a courtroom and from there, ultimately a prison cell. She wrote letters to television shows and psychics and mediums. She hired a host of private investigators who delivered not much more than a bunch of confident promises and handfuls of painstaking invoices.

Every few years, Taft said that she is contacted by someone who was at the party the night that Jamee vanished and that that person usually indicates that they know more about her daughter's circumstances than they are willing to share, then citing myriad reasons to not be more forthcoming.

"There was a girl who came to me a few years back to try to help because she was in the same group and went to prison for drugs," said Taft. "But apparently her probation officer wouldn't let her get involved. I have not reached out to her since, but the thought is in my mind."

CALVIN ZIMDARS

VANISHED: NOVEMBER 29, 2017

VANISHED FROM: GLEN

CALVIN ZIMDARS DIDN'T LEAVE a good-bye or suicide note or hint of where he could have gone. He didn't say good-bye to his children or grandchildren. He didn't close out his bank accounts. He loved his horse and his ranch and bemoaned and bellyached anytime he had to leave the premises or be gone for too long.

Calvin's ranch on Sugarloaf Mountain Road in Glen, Montana, was his castle. At first, his family thought that he might have gone hiking in the nearby hills or mountains. It wasn't unusual for him to explore and lose track of the hours. He was well-acquainted with the country of the Grasshopper Valley surrounding his home and enjoyed fishing, hunting, hiking, and running cattle.

"My husband, Charlie, was Calvin's oldest son," said Dawn Zimdars, his former daughter-in-law. "I met him for the first time in 2006. He grew up in Big Timber and grew up on a farm. He has several brothers and sisters and extended family who still live in the area. He graduated from high school and started working in the oil industry. He was a cowboy. He liked to ride and be involved in rodeo. Saddle broncing and bareback and team roping he participated in the most."

Divorced, he had three grown children, with whom he was exceptionally close.

MISSING

CALVIN CHARLES ZIMDARS, 56

Calvin was last seen at home in Glen, Montana (between Butte and Dillon) on November 30, 2017. He may have gone hiking in the area around his home on Sugarloaf Mountain Road or in the Grasshopper Valley area. Search and rescue operations have failed to located him.

Calvin is at risk of self-harm. He may wear glasses. He has graying hair and blue eyes. He is 5'5"-5'7" and 150-170 pounds. He most often wears Western-style clothing.

Anyone with information should call the Beaverhead County Sheriff's Office at 406-683-3700 or 406-683-2383.

f /MissingNorthwest
🐦 @MissingNW

Calvin Zimdars vanished one day (* after poster circulated the family determined he'd been missing since Nov. 29) in November 2017, and his family alleges that Calvin's fate is linked to a long-standing feud with his neighbor, Randy Brooks. The Beaverhead County sheriff searched Brooks's property and is actively investigating Calvin's disappearance. The Zimdars family has filed a wrongful death lawsuit against Brooks.

"Charlie always said that his dad was there for all of his events," said Dawn. "He coached Charlie's rural basketball league in Polaris. Calvin was the fun guy. He was the dad that was there."

Authorities said that at the time of his disappearance Zimdars, who had been having personal problems, was despondent and may not have intended to return home. He turned his horse out to graze, an indication he planned to be gone for an extended time period. Both his vehicles were left behind at his residence, indicating that most likely if he left of his own volition, he left on foot.

POLICE OPEN TO THEORIES

VERY LITTLE INFORMATION has been shared publicly about the Zimdars case, although Beaverhead County officials said they were open to all ideas and scenarios.

"We would believe that he walked off into the woods, and we would believe that he met with foul play," said a representative of the Beaverhead County Sheriff's Office. "Calvin wasn't the friendliest guy, and he had an ongoing fight with one of his neighbors. But he also was fired from a job recently, and his family said that he might have been suicidal. You take your pick. Murder or suicide?"

Initially, the family told authorities that Calvin was, in fact, distressed and perhaps even suicidal.

"We were at home, and it was later in the evening," said Dawn. "I thought maybe he rode his horse somewhere. Sometimes he could head off and go out of town, and he might not tell you. He'd go roping and flying in his friend's aircraft and go on one of his adventures. He wasn't at his house or the local bar. So where did he go? It's harder now for me to believe he committed suicide because there are so many other weird things that don't add up."

His daughter, Clarissa, said that she now regrets even supplying the information to the police about her dad's low mental state, and that it might have been a mistake to do so because it has gotten authorities fixated on the likelihood. It is highly inconceivable to her that her father would desert his family and friends at his own hand.

"My brother Charlie committed suicide, and we saw the signs, and we tried to get him help," said Clarissa Zimdars. "Dad would not have done that. My dad had a lot to live for. He loved his grandkids. They were his life. The original posters said that he was experiencing possible suicidal thoughts, and that's a problem because that's the only assumption in anyone's mind now."

On the afternoon of Monday, November 27, 2017, Calvin's son, Jay, drove to his ranch to check in with his father. Calvin had recently been released for unclear reasons from his job, "cowboy work on the side," as Clarissa described it. Calvin didn't like being unemployed and worse, he particularly disliked feeling idle, feeling unwanted and purposeless.

"From what I understand, the conversation was not enlightening, and it was a very dark conversation," said Dawn. "Jay said, I'll come back out to check on you on Friday, and Friday came, and there was no dad."

On Tuesday, things got worse for Calvin when he looked out the window and saw a police cruiser parked in the driveway. Beaverhead County Sheriff Bill Knox spoke with Calvin about a complaint filed by his neighbor, Randy Brooks, alleging animal cruelty. Brooks told Knox that Calvin's horse was starving to death. He told the police that Calvin was a horribly abusive animal owner and that the horse had been beaten, whipped, and was grotesquely emaciated from neglect.

Knox spoke with Calvin, inspected the animal, and determined that Brooks's allegations were insufficient and declined to issue a summons or ticket.

The next day, Charlie and Jay returned once again to check on their father and discovered that he was missing. On the evening of Wednesday, November 29, 2017, for several hours Charlie and Jay walked in the remote areas around the house. Concerned, the sons reported Calvin missing to the sheriff that night.

GRUDGE WITH NEIGHBOR COULD PROVIDE MOTIVE FOR MURDER

THE ZIMDARS FAMILY ALLEGES that Calvin's fate is somehow linked to the specious accusations lodged by his neighbor, Randy Brooks.

"Dad did know it was Randy Brooks who reported him," said Clarissa. "That's a hot iron in the fire when the two had already had animosity toward each other. With the animosity those two had—ten years of being pushed by Randy—I could see dad losing his cool."

A couple of things about the condition of her father's house when he went missing troubled Clarissa immediately, including a table that had a bunch of photos of family and friends neatly arranged. The house had the eerie feeling that it had been inspected or examined or visited by someone who might not have been invited. Perhaps most importantly, a giant cavalry pistol was missing, but the holster was dangling over one of the couch seats.

"Dad's table in the house had things that were set in place in a way that was unusual," said Clarissa. "There were pictures, almost like a shrine, like all of the items had been randomly picked and placed on the table."

The gun has never been located. If Calvin did take his own life, he would have had to commit the act after walking in the forest, presumably with the clunky, cumbersome pistol as the suicide weapon.

"This was a big, eight-inch, cowboy gun, and it's not something you are going to carry and walk with," said Clarissa.

Another thing that bothered Calvin's family was that someone had opened and closed all the gates that allowed their dad's horse to pasture; usually their father only opened all the gates when he planned to be gone for an extended period. If it wasn't Calvin, someone else knew the exact pattern of the property lines and knew the gate points to let the horse come and go, perhaps expecting that Calvin would not be returning. According to Jay's statement to police, he learned that it was Randy Brooks. After Jay asked Randy who had been fidgeting with one of the gates, Brooks told Jay that he was the one. "I was just letting the horses in and out and just being neighborly," Jay quoted Brooks as saying. The horse was grazing healthily, but Calvin was nowhere to be found.

NEIGHBOR IDENTIFIED AS PERSON OF INTEREST

RANDY BROOKS WAS NAMED as a person of interest by the Beaverhead County police officials, but he has never formally been charged with a crime. According to police officials, Brooks and Zimdars were known to have a long simmering and, at times, bitter feud rooted in a host of things, including property boundary disagreements, horse grazing, and the alleged animal abuse and neglect complaint.

Calvin bought the property that he lived on from Randy's son, Timothy B. Brooks and his wife, Donna Brooks, on July 7, 2008. According to papers provided by the Beaverhead County police, Randy Brooks attempted to seize the property, 1029 Sugarloaf Mountain Road, in Glen, on multiple occasions. Randy claimed that his rights to the property, however legally muddled and murky, were in his mind absolute.

It seems that various transactions took place between March 1998 and July 2008, during which time Randy Brooks's property was subdivided and transferred to various persons, resulting in Calvin Zimdars acquiring Remainder Tract 2B of Certificate of Survey No. 1485 FT.

In a letter to Beaverhead Title Company dated December 11, 2011, Randy wrote that "we here by [sic] must inform you of our intentions to take control of all of our legal rights within 30 days (Jan. 15, 2011)." In response, Calvin's attorney, Peter M. Tomaryn, wrote to Brooks on January 12, 2012, refuting the claim.

Based on Tomaryn's analysis of the warranty deeds between Randy and Timothy Brooks, the quit claim deed between the two men, the various certificates of survey, and the subsequent warranty deed from Timothy to Calvin, "I find no legal basis for your claims of any type of interest in the Zimdars' property," wrote Tomaryn.

Tomaryn then asked Brooks that he "cease and desist from making any claims against Mr. Zimdars' property right."

Brooks called the police on several occasions claiming that he owned the covenant to the property and that he had a livestock operation and that he was having problems with Zimdars's dogs; once he phoned because Calvin, Randy said, had told him that he wanted to "bring a house trailer onto the property." During one of the disputes, according to the police report, Randy waved a gun in the air, though he didn't point it at Calvin or threaten him with it.

In the spring of 2018, neighbors reported seeing a concrete truck on the Brooks property, and police reports noted that a foundation was poured for a new garage and sidewalks. Beaverhead County sheriffs said that Randy allowed cadaver smelling dogs on the property. After the disappearance of Calvin Zimdars, Randy and his wife, Ila Mae Brooks, moved to Florence but have since returned to Glen.

BROOKS RETURNS TO HOUSE, PROPERTY WITHOUT PERMISSION

On May 1, 2020, Bill Knox, undersheriff, Beaverhead County Sheriff's Office, placed a game-tracking camera on the Zimdars property to attempt to "capture images of who was entering the property without the owner's permission," he said. Someone had placed buckets of paint inside the vacant house and left tools and sawhorses there. And there was more odd activity: someone even went as far as disassembling fences and gates, removing a doghouse, and cutting off the realtor's lockbox.

On May 4, 2020, according to Knox, Brooks called the sheriff's office and wanted to provide some documents that would explain his rights to a life estate in the Zimdars property. According to Knox, the next day Brooks "admitted that he had entered the property but insisted it was his right to do so." Brooks provided Knox with three copies of the warranty deed dated September 9, 1998. Brooks told Knox that on July

1, 2020, he intended to have the Zimdars house fixed up and would be moving in on that day.

Knox elected to not file criminal charges against Brooks, though it seems as if he had a good case against Brooks for, at the very least, criminal trespass (for entering and exiting the home on multiple occasions) and criminal mischief (for damage done to the fences and realtor's box). The house was eventually sold by the Zimdars family.

"Randy lived right up on the hill above Dad, and they'd had problems with each other from day one," said Clarissa. "They'd had legal run-ins and dad considered him an adult bully and a pest. He tried to take possession of the house, tried to get my dad to get rid of his dogs at the house. It went on and on and on."

The Zimdars family filed a civil lawsuit against Randy Brooks alleging that Brooks is solely and wholly responsible for the wrongful death of their loved one. Perhaps not surprisingly, the lawsuit is harsh and heavy with suspicion, minces no words, and is rife with serious accusations and recriminations.

"His case is open, and we are in the legal process to have him declared deceased on paper," said Clarissa Zimdars. "In my heart and my mind, Randy Brooks is 100 percent responsible for what happened to my dad."

Randy Brooks did not respond to multiple requests to be interviewed. Calvin's son, Charles Zimdars, took his own life on July 25, 2018, at age thirty-six, eight months after his father disappeared.

STEVE KILWEIN

MURDERED: JUNE 13, 2021
MURDER LOCATION: BOZEMAN

STEVE KILWEIN ALWAYS WANTED to live under the vast skies of Montana.

In the mid-1980s the middle-aged father of five, a successful contractor and home builder, left North Dakota and settled in Bozeman, moving his wife and family to a location that he had long romanticized.

"He always wanted to live in Bozeman," said Steve's daughter Karla Hacker. "The saddest part to reconcile is that that town ended up killing him."

On June 13, 2021, Kilwein, seventy-nine, was slain in his own home on an otherwise ordinary Sunday morning. The victim, according to the death certificate, received "multiple chop-type wounds," inflicted to the back of the head.

His family continues to search for resolution and struggles to comprehend that such an irrational act of violence could be inflicted on their loved one without consequence.

"People should know about it," said Karla Hacker. "There's still a killer walking around town, maybe still in Bozeman, someone who brutally murdered our father. Most people have no idea that this happened. We have a $100,000 reward, but there's not an outrage or anything."

"I am still in denial," said his daughter Karen Hamilton. "How could this happen in the town he absolutely loved?"

On June 13, 2021, Steve Kilwein, seventy-nine, was slain in his Bozeman home on an otherwise ordinary Sunday morning. He was the victim, according to the death certificate, of "multiple chop-type wounds" to the back of the head. His family continues to search for resolution and struggles to comprehend how such an irrational act of violence could be inflicted on their loved one without consequence.
COURTESY KARLA HACKER

THE ROAD TO BOZEMAN: A DREAM FULFILLED

STEVE JOSEPH KILWEIN was born in 1941 and raised in Dickinson, North Dakota, the second youngest of thirteen children, five of whom died of sickness or disease before they reached the age of two. His father, Martin Kilwein, of hard-working, German ethnicity, operated a grain, wheat, and flax farm spanning more than six hundred acres south of South Heart and abutting the Badlands.

In his upbringing were homegrown chickens and canned goods; his favored entertainment was chucking marbles with his brother Roger during recess at St. Joe's elementary school, and he didn't experience the comfort of indoor plumbing until the family moved closer to town when he was a teenager.

Steve graduated from Dickinson High School in 1960, and Ron Lisko graduated two years later. Ron, smaller, less physically prominent, idolized the older student, whom he first met after Steve stood up to some ruffians who were bullying him. They were both members of Dickinson High School wrestling teams.

"I was a junior, and I wrestled in the 133-pound class, and Steve was at a higher weight." said Lisko. "He was a strong guy, a leader, with a good personality, someone who could take control of things. He liked to arm wrestle, too, and if you were arm wrestling against Steve, you'd better be in good shape. He'd drive up and down the main drag in a Ford '57 with the driver's side door missing. I thought of him as the Fonz of the south side of Dickinson."

After graduating from high school, he went to work in construction, he and his brother Roger teaming together on countless projects, including drywalling jobs at the campus at Dickinson State College and the Prairie Hills Mall, as well as interior and exterior home painting assignments throughout the Dickinson area.

"For ten or fifteen years it seemed like we worked every night together, and we had a new duplex to start every Monday morning," said Roger Kilwein.

By chance he met Judith Pavlicik at a house party, and the couple dated for two years, married in 1964, and in the end reared five children: Kurt, Karen, Karla, Keith, and Kari.

"Judy was the best person and always positive, and she had the best laugh," said Steve's sister Jeanette Olheiser.

After graduating from Dickinson State College in art and business, Steve taught English at the Job Corps, and served as a drug and alcohol rehabilitation counselor at the state hospital in Jamestown. This type of work softened his heart and instilled an unshakable belief in him that people ought to have second or even third chances. An avid artist, he once found employment painting a local steeple.

"A serial entrepreneur," as described by his son Kurt Kilwein, Steve later worked as a banker and owned a lumberyard and even a saloon. But it was his work as a home builder that brought him the most financial success; he was smart, witty, adept at solving problems quickly and efficiently. Kilwein Construction built a sizable number of houses, subdivisions, and business offices in the Dickinson area.

Many remarked that there was something gentle about him, considerate. His affection was boundless: once, he'd bought a funky little car in the classifieds and left it in the parking lot of the high school for his girls. He'd grinningly walked home, allowing them to discover the gift after tennis practice. His children had friends who lacked father figures, and he would fill such voids with kindness, contributing his time and skill repairing their vehicles.

During the summer months, Steve and Judy packed the Winnebago and took the children to the property that the family had purchased in the Virginia City area of southwest Montana.

The former gold mine became the source of many glossy memories, days spent enjoying exploring the shafts and fissures, and nights at a friend's cabin in Ennis stretched under the stars.

With his three oldest children attending or about to attend Montana State University, Steve saw the opportunity to fulfill his dream of fully living in Montana. It was the summer of 1986 when he and his wife and the youngest two kids moved to Bozeman. After a while the Kilweins purchased a modest home downtown.

"The house used to be purple, so everyone knew the purple house behind Safeway," said his daughter Karen Hamilton.

In retirement, Steve was constantly in motion, chopping timber, hauling tools, laying down and tearing up floors, or tinkering on assorted projects in the garage. He was an avid reader, especially knowledgeable about the crucial events and decisive battles of the Civil War and World War II as well as the life of President Theodore Roosevelt.

He almost always wore baseball caps. One of his favorites was from the Ronald Reagan Presidential Library and Museum, a place Steve visited several times; and another, rimmed with silly plastic bird poop, read "San Pedro Island." He owned caps for all occasions and sports teams: the Minnesota Vikings while in Bozeman and the Denver Broncos when he was in Colorado to visit family.

Soon, all the Kilwein offspring were scattered in three states—Colorado, Washington, and California—and circumstances demanded that he and Judy travel a great deal. When grandkids arrived, it sparked the wonder of a second childhood in Steve, all balloons and party hats and streamers. There were pranks with water balloons and crazy water-gun battles; poker games involving stashes of surplus Halloween candy, with grandpa feigning ruthlessness while allowing them to win and deplete his supply; surprise attacks from the closet with a rushing volley of foam Nerf balls.

Steve and Judy took to traveling and exploring the seminal landmarks and battlefields around the nation, including Thomas Jefferson's Monticello and Appomattox, as well as cruising, embarking on multiple trips to destinations such as Alaska, Panama, the Caribbean, and the Mediterranean.

"Watching Steve and Judy was like watching two people who were in love," said Steve's sister Leona Moriarty. "They giggled all the time, and they were good parents."

SUMMER 2021: HEART STILL TIED
TO BOZEMAN

COME THE SUMMER OF 2021, Steve Kilwein, seventy-nine, was still adjusting to a life as a widower. Judith Kilwein had passed away from heart failure in June 2019, at age seventy-five. Before she died, the couple had lived in a house in the Denver area, a few doors away from one of their children and grandchildren. Judy embraced the move wholeheartedly, but Steve wouldn't cut his connection to Bozeman, spending time in both places.

He had a sore, stiff back, which in the past had required three separate surgeries, and he would sometimes need the assistance of a cane. He was in remission from prostate cancer. Nonetheless, he was just as quick and capable showing an interested party how to properly insulate a house or hang sheetrock or tape and texture drywall as he had been in his thirties. The yard was littered with disheveled automobiles, including a 1949 Ford, and Steve's latest interior remodeling job gave the property the appearance of an active construction zone.

He had a crew of buddies he met at Rosauers supermarket more or less daily for coffee, and practically every afternoon he visited Home Depot or Lowe's, where he chatted amiably with employees, many of whom he knew by name.

Invariably decked out in blue jeans, a flannel shirt, and a baseball cap, Kilwein never passed up an opportunity to initiate a conversation or make people laugh with silly, unselfconscious jokes.

Saturday, June 12, 2021. The day was hot and bright; cumulus clouds like mountains loomed in the sky. Steve purchased moving boxes to pack up more things to transfer to Colorado. He had made no plans to sell the house in

Bozeman, explaining to his children that he still found beauty there, and it gave his life some meaning.

"We tried to get him to put the last of the stuff in the truck," said Karla Hacker. "It was his choice to stay there. He kept saying he was going to move. But we couldn't get him out of Bozeman. He loved it."

One of his daughters spoke with him late in the evening. He told her that he was going to make soup or fix a sandwich and then retire to bed. He said he planned to mow the yard the following morning.

Sunday, June 13, 2021. At approximately 11 a.m., as the sun burned its way higher in the sky, something horrible happened to Steve Kilwein.

He did not answer his cell phone. After numerous unsuccessful attempts, one of his children contacted the Bozeman Police Department at about 9 p.m.

"It would have been odd to be out of contact with him for more than twelve hours," said his daughter Kari Gray. "The second none of us had heard from him, we knew something was wrong; perhaps he fell or he'd gotten hurt. The policeman said, your father is deceased. And then we heard from the coroner Monday morning, who said he was electrocuted."

Law enforcement's initial diagnosis of an accidental death by electrocution struck his children as strangely implausible.

"He was an experienced contractor, and he owned a construction company, and there was no way he would have touched a live wire," said Karla Hacker.

"He was a smart man, and he could build a house from scratch, and we knew there was no way that my dad accidentally electrocuted himself," said Hamilton.

Still, the Kilwein children were prepared to accept such a scenario as the cause of their father's death. After all, he was constantly tearing apart dividing walls, removing partitions, rebuilding panels. Did an unprotected thread of wires freakishly shock him?

Then Tuesday morning, one of the Kilwein children received a call from a Bozeman detective asking for permission to enter Steve's house. Soon, the line of questioning from the police turned noticeably more serious.

"The questioning became odd for somebody who's been electrocuted," said Kari. "And that's when the detective said that they were looking at other possibilities."

CLASSIFIED AS HOMICIDE

ON TUESDAY, JUNE 15, 2021, the Bozeman Police Department issued a curt press release addressing the fate of Steve Kilwein.

"The Bozeman police classified it as a homicide on Tuesday morning," said Karla Hacker. "The news release from the police department said that it was someone known to him and that there was no threat to the general public."

"All the police said was that it was someone he knew, and they had a strong suspect, and that made you think that there'd be an arrest soon," said Roger Kilwein. "That didn't happen."

Details remain stubbornly minimal, though the death certificate identifies "multiple chop-type wounds" as the cause of death, "implying a hatchet or ax," suggested Kurt Kilwein, though the instrument or tool of violence has never been made public.

Over the years Steve had experienced several thefts from his residence, unique bits and pieces, such as a World War I combat helmet, which he quickly recovered at the neighboring pawnshop. A Swiss watch had disappeared from inside the house just days before. But Steve's construction and lawn tools were left untouched, including a table saw, a nail gun, and an air compressor.

On Sunday morning, June 13, 2021, around 11 a.m., Steve's lawn mower was filled with gas, positioned a few feet from the front door. None of the locks or doors showed damage, and there were no signs of a break-in or vandalism. Steve's wallet was found in his bedroom, containing approximately $2,300 from the sale of a Suburban.

The autopsy report indicated that a struggle transpired and Steve, still physically prominent at six feet, two inches, about 200 pounds, might even have fought with his attacker. No one heard or saw anything suspicious on that quiet block in that quiet neighborhood.

Built in 1910 or earlier, Kilwein's modest single-family home at 101 North Ninth Avenue, approximately 742 square feet, is located on a one-way street neighboring Summit Church at 921 W. Mendenhall Street. The house is just two blocks from Bozeman High School on 11th Avenue.

"Church would have been in session when my dad was killed," said Karen Hamilton. "Someone brutally attacked him and then coldly and callously just walked out the front door, and that person is potentially still walking around Bozeman."

Friendliness and chattiness were two of Steve's trademarks and so, too, was compassion. Recently, there was a downtrodden drifter who, Steve learned, liked to repair cars. Steve had found odd jobs for the man fixing various engine parts, until one day Steve stepped on a crack pipe in the backyard. Refusing to tolerate any drug use on his property, Steve sent the man on his way. It's unclear whether police have ever considered the man as a suspect.

"I think we all think that it was probably someone he knew," said Kari. "He never locked his door in the day. He was kind of always adopting people, and in the past, he had an old trailer; he had people living in the trailer in the back."

"Could my dad's generosity and caring nature be what eventually took his life from him?" asked Karen Hamilton.

Ironically, Steve wasn't even supposed to be in Montana on the day he was murdered: an appointment in Colorado to have MRI scans of a sore hand and neck had been rescheduled.

Days later he was buried. Solemnity with a pat of sunshine: each of the five children would wear one of their father's baseball caps in remembrance. When they laid him to rest, they did not know that his murderer would remain faceless, and the police search would be fruitless.

Steve's loved ones find the adage about time healing all wounds to be untrue. Grief doesn't grow fainter: its shell hardens, and it aches in new ways. They will spend the anniversary cleaning his grave. Compounding their pain is the perception some of Steve's children held that the murder of their father is obsolete news or perhaps even worse, not news at all.

"From the start, his murder has been treated as if he were just an old guy living in a torn-apart house," said Karla Hacker. "But there was so much more to him. He had beautiful grandkids who he adored. He had a loving wife for fifty-five years. Had he been in one of the million-dollar homes in Bozeman and not scruffy looking, would the outcome of this case have been different?"

A $100,000 reward is available for information leading to the arrest and conviction of the person or persons responsible for the murder of Steve Kilwein. Anyone with information about his homicide can contact Detective Ben King at (406) 582-2242 or email crimetips@bozeman.net.

INDEX

ABOUT THE AUTHOR

Brian D'Ambrosio is a prolific writer of nonfiction and author of several books. As a freelancer, he covers a wide range of topics, from cold cases to musician profiles to articles about the lives and talents of eccentric artists. He was nominated for numerous awards for *Warrior in the Ring* in 2014 and several independent publishing awards for *Life in the Trenches* (2014). He lives in Helena, Montana, and Santa Fe, New Mexico. He may be reached at dambrosiobrian@hotmail.com.

ALSO BY BRIAN D'AMBROSIO

SELECTED WORKS

From Haikus to Hatmaking: One Year in the Life of Western Montana

Free Ryan Ferguson: 101 Reasons Why Ryan Should Be Released

Warrior in the Ring: The Life of Marvin Camel, American Indian World Champion Boxer

Shot in Montana: A History of Big Sky Cinema

Montana and the NFL

Montana Entertainers: Famous and Almost Forgotten

Montana Murders: Notorious and Unsolved

Montana Eccentrics: A Collection of Extraordinary Montanans, Past and Present